MCDP 3

Expeditionary Operations

U.S. Marine Corps

DEPARTMENT OF THE NAVY
Headquarters United States Marine Corps
Washington, D.C. 20380-1775

16 April 1998

FOREWORD

Marine Corps Doctrinal Publication (MCDP) 3, *Expeditionary Operations*, establishes doctrine for the conduct of military operations by the U.S. Marine Corps. It describes the Marine Corps as an expeditionary force-in-readiness that is manned, trained, and equipped specifically to respond quickly to a broad variety of crises and conflicts across the full range of military operations anywhere in the world. It emphasizes the naval character of Marine Corps forces. This naval expeditionary character provides capabilities both to forward-deploy forces near the scene of potential crises as well as to deploy sustainable, combined arms teams rapidly by sea and air. With reduced overseas presence in terms of force levels and bases, these capabilities have become essential elements of our national military strategy. This publication also underscores the value of Marine Corps forces as a highly cost-effective option in a wide range of situations, including crises requiring forcible entry. Importantly, this publication establishes versatility and adaptability as critical capabilities in a broad range of circumstances for expeditionary forces in an uncertain world. Finally, this publication describes the Marine Corps' key expeditionary concepts.

This publication is compatible with the Marine Corps' capstone doctrinal publication, MCDP 1, *Warfighting*. *Warfighting* provides the broad institutional and operating philosophy that underlies all Marine Corps expeditionary operations, regardless of echelon of command or operating setting. This publication applies that philosophy more specifically to the operations of Marine air-ground task forces (MAGTFs) and to the types of expeditionary settings in which these forces will likely be required to operate. Where MCDP 1 describes the Marine Corps' philosophy of warfighting, this publication describes the types of operations of which Marine Corps forces must be capable.

Chapter 1 describes the complex and uncertain geopolitical environment near the turn of the 21st century—the environment in which Marine Corps forces will be required to operate. Based on chapter 1, chapter 2 establishes the need for a flexible, naval expeditionary force-in-readiness, describes the requirements of expeditionary operations, and identifies the characteristics and capabilities of Marine Corps forces that satisfy those requirements. Chapter 3 describes the particular expeditionary organizations and forces that the Marine Corps contributes in support of national interests overseas. Chapter 4 describes the operating concepts that underlie the Marine Corps' conduct of expeditionary operations. Key among these is the naval concept, operational maneuver from the sea.

This publication is designed for Marine Corps leaders who must conduct expeditionary operations or advise others on the effective employment of Marine Corps forces and for those outside the Marine Corps who must understand Marine Corps capabilities and operating concepts. Because this publication describes concepts that are fundamental to Marine Corps operations, it is required reading for all Marines.

C. C. KRULAK
General, U.S. Marine Corps
Commandant of the Marine Corps

DISTRIBUTION: 142 000009 00

Throughout this publication, masculine nouns and pronouns are used for the sake of simplicity. Except where otherwise noted, these nouns and pronouns apply to either gender.

Expeditionary Operations

Chapter 1. The Landscape: Chaos in the Littorals

After the Cold War: The "New Anarchy"—Crises: Disaster, Disruption, Dispute—Fragmentation and Integration—Major Regional Contingency—Smaller-Scale Contingencies— Nonstate Actors—The Developing World—Population Factors—Urbanized Terrain—The Importance of the Sea and the Littoral Regions—Weaponry—Conclusion

Chapter 2. The Nature of Expeditionary Operations

National Interests, Crisis Prevention, and Crisis Response— Expeditionary Operations Defined and Discussed—Reasons for Conducting Expeditionary Operations—Sequence in Projecting Expeditionary Forces—Expeditionary Mindset— Naval Character—Strategic Mobility: Closure Rate and Global Reach—Operational Mobility—Operational and Tactical Competence—Sustainability—Adaptability— Reconstitution—Cost-Effectiveness—Conclusion

Chapter 3. Expeditionary Organizations

Naval Expeditionary Forces—Marine Corps Forces Commands—Marine Air-Ground Task Forces—

The Structure of the MAGTF—The Marine Expeditionary
Force—The Marine Expeditionary Unit (Special Operations
Capable)—The Special Purpose MAGTF—Maritime
Prepositioning Forces—Air Contingency Forces—
Marine Component Commands—Standing Task Force
Headquarters—Conclusion

Chapter 4.   Expeditionary Concepts

Operational Maneuver from the Sea—Case Study: The
Marianas, 1944—Sustained Operations Ashore—Case
Study: The Persian Gulf, 1990–1991—Military Operations
Other Than War—Case Study: Mogadishu, Somalia,
1991—Maritime Prepositioning Force Operations—Case
Study: Saudi Arabia, 1990—Conclusion

Epilogue.   Operation Littoral Chaos

Case Study: West Africa, 2017–18—Conclusion

Notes

Chapter 1

The Landscape: Chaos in the Littorals

"It must be considered that there is nothing more difficult to carry out, nor more doubtful of success, nor more dangerous to handle, than to initiate a new order of things."[1]

—Niccolo Machiavelli

". . . a second Cold War might be upon us—a protracted struggle between ourselves and the demons of crime, population pressure, environmental degradation, disease, and culture conflict."[2]

—Robert D. Kaplan

T his chapter discusses the environment in which U.S. forces in general, and Marine Corps expeditionary forces in particular, have to operate. It describes a world characterized by disorder and crisis, especially in the littoral regions of the developing world.

AFTER THE COLD WAR: THE "NEW ANARCHY"

The end of the Cold War has ushered in a period of widespread uncertainty, rapid change, and turmoil. The Cold War provided a known enemy whom we thought we understood fairly well and against whom we could prepare. The Cold War provided structure and stability. The global ideological struggle between the United States and the Soviet Union tended to subsume lesser, regional conflicts. As local belligerents positioned themselves on opposing sides of the Cold War, local conflicts were overshadowed by the global struggle and were often suppressed out of fear of starting a global war.

The certainty, structure, and stability that the Cold War provided have disappeared. The geopolitical situation has shifted from a bipolar global structure to multiple regional power centers with a single world superpower—the United States. Conflict has arisen as political groups vie for regional dominance. Long-simmering animosities have erupted into conflict. In short, the threat has shifted from the known enemies of the

3

Cold War to a broader, heterogeneous set of potential competitors and adversaries and a variety of types of conflict. Some of these opponents are traditional nation-states, but many will be nonstate actors—such as terrorist groups and international organized crime networks—that present new and unique challenges.

The political map of the world is changing quickly, and the trend seems likely to continue for the foreseeable future. Democracy and capitalism continue to spread across the globe, although the transition is hardly a smooth or peaceful one. Where democracy has newly taken hold, its survival is not assured. For that matter, democratic states are not necessarily peaceful states. At the same time, anti-Western sentiment, especially anti-American sentiment, thrives in many parts of the world. According to one noted political scientist, the ideological clash of the Cold War will be replaced by a "clash of civilizations."[3] The perception of the U.S.'s political, economic, and military dominance, reinforced by the military results of the Gulf War, will lead many potential enemies to adopt asymmetrical methods that avoid our material and technological superiority and exploit our perceived weaknesses. Along with other asymmetrical forms of political violence, terrorism will continue to pose a threat to U.S. citizens, property, and interests and will remain difficult to combat.

Dangerous combinations of demographic, economic, and social forces threaten to overwhelm resources, infrastructure, and governmental control in many parts of the world. As a result, the need for humanitarian assistance will continue to grow in the foreseeable future. According to one estimate, humanitarian crises today are four times more frequent, last longer, and cause more damage than in the 1980s.[4] This is especially true in the developing world, although not exclusively. Several established states have demonstrated surprising instability and currently face the prospect of great change and uncertain futures.

While threats to national security may have decreased in order of magnitude, they have increased in number, frequency, and variety. These lesser threats have proven difficult to ignore. The main point of this discussion is to point out that the post-Cold War geopolitical situation has fundamentally altered the nature and scope of future military conflicts. This situation requires a diverse range of military methods and capabilities for effective response. Far from creating a new world order, the end of the Cold War has led to what former United Nations Secretary-General Perez de Cuellar has described as the "new anarchy."[5]

CRISES: DISASTER, DISRUPTION, DISPUTE

In short, the end of the Cold War has resulted in a world characterized by widespread disorder and potential crisis.[6] In the coming years, the ability to respond effectively and quickly to crises will be essential to the protection of U.S. interests. Crises that will threaten U.S. interests in the near future fall into three broad categories: disasters, disruptions, and disputes.[7]

Disasters are accidents or calamities—complex human emergencies—that cause suffering on a massive scale. Disasters create societal and political instability as well as physical devastation. If a disaster reaches significant enough proportions without an effective government response, it may lead to violence and even rebellion. Disasters may be natural or manmade. Natural disasters are the best known and include hurricanes, tornadoes, earthquakes, floods, droughts, plagues, epidemics, and wildfires. Less frequent but sometimes even more destructive are manmade disasters such as nuclear or other industrial accidents, economic failures, or catastrophic governmental collapse.

The second class of crisis is disruption. Disruptions are intentionally disorderly activities that cause internal commotion on a scale sufficient to interfere with a government's ability to perform its functions. Unlike disasters, which are generally the result of the forces of nature or unintentional human actions, disruptions are the result of human intent. These may be the actions of an organized political group with a unified agenda such as an insurgency movement or terrorist organization, a criminal organization more interested in profits than politics such as a drug cartel, or an accumulation of individuals or small groups acting in their own self-interest. The effects of disruptions are internal to the country in question, although the disruptive element itself may originate externally or receive external support. Disruptions may include genocide, terrorism, insurgency, drug trafficking, and epidemic crime. They may stem from sectarianism, nationalism, racial or religious hatred, or extreme poverty. Disasters can lead to disruption if there is widespread dissatisfaction with the government response to the disaster.

The third class of crisis is dispute, a clash between two political groups. A disruption may escalate to a dispute when the disruptive element becomes powerful enough to openly challenge the established government rather than to merely subvert its authority. Disputes may be internal, as in a rebellion or insurrection, or external between sovereign states or other independent political groups. A dispute may result from a single incident, or it may be a lasting ethnic, ideological, or other difference. It may take the form of political tension that does not generally result in military violence—such as the Cold War—or it may result in open warfare that may itself take any number of forms and intensities.

The intent here is not to try to categorize every type of political crisis. The point is simply that in a broad range of situations potentially threatening to U.S. interests, the actual or contemplated commitment of U.S. military forces will arise. The actual U.S. response will depend on the situation.

FRAGMENTATION AND INTEGRATION

Two of the primary forces that drive changes in global politics are the simultaneous processes of fragmentation and integration, which one noted political scientist has described as "fragmegration."[8] These processes contribute significantly to the complexity and unpredictability of current world events.

A main trend in global politics is fragmentation: the breakup of multination states into smaller, more natural national groups with narrower communities of interest. Since 1990, the trend toward fragmentation has been unmistakable. This trend reflects the failure of some states to satisfy the political needs of all their constituents. It also reflects the tendency of groups to define their interests more narrowly than before. This fragmentation is rarely a smooth process. The existing state usually resists the loss of authority. Moreover, the drawing of boundaries and the creation of other arrangements can rarely be done to the satisfaction of all concerned parties. The simple increase in the number of active political groups as a result of fragmentation increases the complexity of global political relations because the interests of some different groups invariably overlap and conflict.

A second major trend in global relations is integration. At the same time that the world is fragmenting politically, it is becoming increasingly connected economically through the rise in global markets. This economic integration results largely from advances in communications technologies that provide both near-instantaneous worldwide transfer of capital and worldwide access to goods and services. As a simple example, one popular "American" basketball shoe is actually assembled from 52 different components that come from five different countries, and it is shipped by sea or air to markets all over the world.[9] The United States has significant commercial interests worldwide. Some of them, such as Persian Gulf oil, are clearly vital to national interests while others, such as the basketball shoe industry, are important but not vital. Another manifestation of increased interconnectedness may be the current decline of unilateral action and the rise of consensus-building among governments before applying military force.

The result of simultaneous fragmentation and integration is a tightly coupled, increasingly complex global social-political system that is potentially very sensitive to disruptions and in which seemingly local events in one part of the world can have potentially significant effects elsewhere.

MAJOR REGIONAL CONTINGENCY

At the high end of the range of potential crises is the threat posed by major regional contingencies. At present, the United States is the single nation on the globe that possesses a military capability to unilaterally protect and pursue its interests worldwide. This condition is likely to be the case for the immediate future, but if history is any guide, it is unlikely to be permanent. At some time in the future, another power—whether an existing state, a new state, an alliance of states, or some other political entity—is likely to rise up to challenge the United States on roughly equal military and other terms.

Despite the current absence of a global peer competitor, the world remains an uncertain and dangerous place, and the United States faces a number of significant challenges to its security. Several regions, including the Korean peninsula and the Mideast, are areas of continuous political tension with a more or less permanent threat of hostilities. Numerous regional powers are capable of temporarily challenging U.S. supremacy regionally and compelling the United States to make a significant commitment of military forces to establish superiority. Several regional powers hostile to, or at least not friendly toward, the United States maintain large militaries with offensive capability in relatively high states of readiness. They may not be equipped with the very latest technology, but they may compensate with quantity for what they lack in quality. Furthermore, some of these powers have demonstrated a tolerance for casualties that to some extent offsets the technological superiority of U.S. forces. Several regional powers possess nuclear weapons, and more have chemical and biological weapons.

These powers may attack U.S. forces, activities, or interests directly in a region, but a more likely scenario is a clash between regional powers that threatens U.S. interests. Although a third party to such conflicts, the United States may find itself bound by treaty obligations or may feel pressure from the world community to intervene as a major member of an international coalition.

A direct military conflict with a major power is an unlikely event—at least for the foreseeable future—but it would be the conflict most threatening to our national interests and security. It would be the one eventuality that poses a direct threat to national survival, and so we must be prepared to protect against it. Such a conflict could involve, among other things, intense conventional combat with advanced weaponry and large military formations. Such a conflict could be protracted and would likely involve a period of mobilization and deployment of forces. The initial clashes, however, could occur unexpectedly and would almost certainly involve the rapid commitment of forward units that must therefore maintain the capability to fight such wars.

SMALLER-SCALE CONTINGENCIES

While major regional contingencies pose the gravest threat to national security, the most likely and most frequent crises into which the United States will find itself drawn will be smaller-scale contingencies involving military operations other than war. Environmental disasters, insurrections, separatist movements, rebellions, coups, genocide, and general societal and governmental collapse all generate violence and instability that may not lead to major regional contingencies but may nonetheless threaten U.S. interests. U.S. commitments in these situations may include presence, civil support, counterdrug operations, peace building and peacekeeping, counterinsurgency, and noncombatant evacuation operations.

Smaller-scale contingencies may involve combat with regular, or conventional, military forces. Most militaries in the developing world are organized and equipped primarily to maintain internal order or for defense, and they lack a power-projection capability. Some of these conventional forces may have advanced weapons and equipment, but usually they use predominantly older equipment, often purchased as surplus from major powers that are upgrading their own arsenals. They tend to use inexpensive weapons systems that are easy to maintain, sustain, and operate rather than expensive, high-technology platforms, but they may invest in high technology in certain areas like air defense, command and control, etc. Included in this category are explosive mines, both land and sea, that can be as effective as they are inexpensive and widespread. The rampant and unrecorded use of mines can take a horrible toll on combatants and civilian populations and can pose a threat for generations.

Conversely, smaller-scale contingencies frequently also involve clashes with unconventional military or paramilitary organizations—criminal and drug rings, vandals and looters, militias, guerrillas, terrorist organizations, urban gangs—that blur the distinction between war and widespread criminal violence.[10] These organizations are likely to employ unconventional weapons and techniques—even relatively simple and cheap weapons of mass destruction—that provide a challenging asymmetrical response to a superior conventional capability. The weapons our future foes most often choose to employ against us may bear little resemblance to today's conventional weapons.

Even noncombat missions such as humanitarian assistance that do not involve a clearly identified enemy are not necessarily undertaken in a permissive environment. U.S. forces performing such missions may find themselves operating in a lawless environment dominated by the threat of violence. The operating environment often fluctuates between permissive and hostile, and protection of the force is invariably a key consideration.

NONSTATE ACTORS

Although the state remains the predominant entity in global politics, its preeminence in the use of organized political violence has declined. One of the trends of modern conflict is the rise of powerful nonstate groups able and willing to apply force on a scale sufficient to have noticeable political effect. This rise of nonstate actors is one of the manifestations of the political fragmentation discussed earlier. The result is a decline in conventional interstate warfare. According to 1996 United Nations statistics, of the 82 conflicts started since the fall of the Berlin Wall in 1989, only three were conventional wars between states; 79 were civil wars or insurgencies involving at least one nonstate belligerent.[11]

Many of these nonstate groups employ unconventional military methods and weapons because they cannot compete with established states in conventional military terms. They are likely not to abide by the laws and conventions of warfare recognized by states. They are especially unlikely to be willing to meet an industrialized military power like the United States on its own terms but will probably adopt methods specifically intended to counter the conventional material and technological superiority of their foe. As a result, they are often difficult to target militarily. Furthermore, lack of political accountability makes them less vulnerable to political, diplomatic, and economic pressure than established states.

Nonstate groups are most likely to have significant influence in smaller-scale contingencies, especially internal con- flicts, but this influence is not restricted to participation in smaller-scale contingencies. Some nonstate powers may wield significant influence in larger conflicts as well.

THE DEVELOPING WORLD

The most volatile regions of the globe—the most likely scenes of crisis requiring U.S. involvement—are generally not in the industrialized world, but in the developing world. These are generally the regions undergoing the greatest change. They are often regions afflicted by drought, disease, and ages-old ethnic hatreds. Government institutions lack stability, and many suffer from internal corruption.

Some of the most rapidly growing regions in the world usually lack the economy, infrastructure, and government institutions needed to deal with that rapid growth. Some of the most densely populated regions on earth often suffer severe resource shortages. Competition for scarce resources— whether basic necessities such as food, water, and shelter or strategic resources that can bring prosperity—can lead to conflict.

Under these conditions, practically any crisis can result in mass refugee movement. The cause of this movement varies—it may be famine, genocide, internal warfare, conventional war, lack of work, or political oppression. "Worldwide, the UN estimates there are more than 17 million refugees— 10,000 people a day forced to leave their countries for fear of persecution and violence—and there are more than 30 mil-lion internally displaced persons within certain countries. Refugees and displaced persons bring their frustrations, disappointments, fears, and grievances with them. They impose a logistical and financial burden upon their hosts."[12] Refugees introduce humanitarian and often political issues into any military intervention, complicating the conduct of military operations. In fact, refugee management may itself be the primary objective of an operation.

Lack of modern or developed infrastructure can pose significant problems for military action in the developing world. Many ports cannot handle the deepest-draft ships. Many airfields in the developing world cannot handle the largest military transport aircraft. Many roads and bridges cannot accommodate military traffic.

The developing world often lacks the capability to cope with major disasters and disruptions—or to deal with the refugee migrations that these cause. Developing countries often lack the military might to resist invasion from without or insurrection from within. Thus, it is in the developing world that American forces will most likely find themselves committed to protect national interests.

POPULATION FACTORS

Conflict is at base a clash of human interests. Conflict arises where there is discontent, where conditions are in flux, and where resources are in short supply. Uncontrolled population growth in the developing world increases competition for the basic necessities of life. Nearly all of this growth will be in Asia, Latin America, and Africa, some of the poorest regions of the world.[13] While in the developed world populations will age without significant growth, populations in the developing world will continue to increase dramatically for the foreseeable future. (See figure.) This rate of increase alone will increase the competition for resources and the likelihood of conflict.

Rapid population growth will likely lead to two demographic phenomena with major security implications: urbaniza-

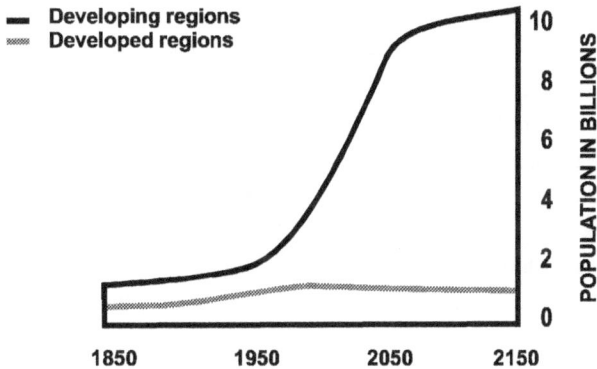

World population trends.

tion and a "youth bulge."[14] As the population continues to grow, more people move to the cities. Today, 45 percent of the world's population—2.5 billion people—lives in cities. At projected rates, the world's urban population will double—to 5

17

billion—by 2025, making 61 percent of the entire world's population urban dwellers.[15]

As recently as 1950, widespread urbanization was a distinction of the industrialized world. Today urban areas are increasingly a feature of the developing world. Of the cities of more than a million people, two-thirds are now in the developing world. As much as 90 percent of the world's population growth will occur in the cities of the developing world.[16]

A rapidly increasing population becomes proportionately younger than a stable population. This youth bulge stresses governments and societies in two mutually reinforcing ways. First, children are relatively unproductive members of society, consumers rather than producers of goods. They must be supported by the society. Second, youth in many cultures are impatient for change and thus more likely to favor radical, even violent, solutions to societal problems. Because of the youth bulge, an increasingly large part of the population in the developing world will be both unproductive and prone to disruptive behavior.

From the basic needs of food, water, and shelter to the industrial requirements for raw materials and energy, more people require more resources. However, population growth will most likely occur in just those areas least able to support burgeoning populations. The disadvantaged, deprived, and dissatisfied are likely to fight for what they think they must have or to try to move where they think they can get it. Groups may resort to war over control of resources, and factions able to control resources will gain disproportionate influence over central governments.[17]

URBANIZED TERRAIN

Urbanization has significant environmental effects. As the earth's urban population increases, so does the proportion of the earth's surface given over to urbanization. As the earth's population becomes increasingly urban, so do tomorrow's likely battlefields. Currently, only about 1 percent of the earth's surface is urbanized terrain. However, urban areas are rapidly expanding. Nearly 1.2 million acres of arable land in developing regions are transformed to urban use annually.[18]

These burgeoning cities are not the organized, high-rise cities of the industrialized world. Large parts are spontaneous shanty or squatter settlements that tend to grow much more rapidly and haphazardly than the rest of a city. These unplanned sprawls can swell to huge dimensions, becoming "unintended" cities in themselves, technically within the boundaries of a metropolitan area but beyond the control of local government and without any organized infrastructure.[19]

Urbanized terrain has significant military implications. It favors the defender over the attacker and the local over an expeditionary force. It often poses significant security problems for

19

a foreign intervention. While training for military operations on urbanized terrain has focused on the difficulties posed by modern multistory urban areas (to include subterranean levels), some of the most challenging areas will be the shanty slums spreading quickly through and around modern cities. These closely packed and densely populated warrens of transient populations, temporary structures, and no organized design can pose greater military problems than modern urban areas.

Combat in urbanized areas is both costly and time consuming. Urbanized terrain tends to complicate the employment of armor, artillery, and close air support. The presence of a non-combatant population provides concealment for indigenous combatants or disruptive elements and can restrict the employment of heavy weapons. Whether the mission is one of humanitarian aid, peacekeeping, or combat, urban terrain favors the use of ground forces, especially infantry, because the use of mechanized forces is often restricted. Moreover, because of the compartmentalized nature of the terrain, an urban battlefield can absorb much greater numbers of troops than open terrain. Combat tends to take place at extremely short range between small units, leading to greater reliance on small-unit leadership and proficiency.

THE IMPORTANCE OF THE SEA AND THE LITTORAL REGIONS

The sea dominates the surface of our globe. Despite the availability of transoceanic aircraft, most international trade is carried by sea. More than 99.5 percent of all overseas cargo by weight travels in ships, and total world seaborne trade continues to increase.[20] A standard 30-knot transport ship can outlift even the largest transport aircraft in weight of cargo by roughly 200:1.[21] The undeniable conclusion is that, for the foreseeable future, there is no viable alternative to shipping by sea for the overwhelming preponderance of world commerce.

The world's littoral regions, where land and sea meet, are equally important. The littorals are where seaborne trade originates and enters its markets. The littorals include straits, most of the world's population centers, and the areas of maximum growth. Straits represent strategic chokepoints from which the world's sea lanes of communications can be controlled. Population centers are focal points of both trade and conflict. Some 60 percent of the world's population lives within 100 kilometers of the ocean. Some 70 percent lives within 320 kilometers. By far the most cities with populations of more than one million are located in the littorals.[22] Coastal cities—that is, cities directly adjacent to the sea—are home to almost a billion people worldwide and are experiencing unprecedented growth. Again, much of this growth is occurring in developing regions. Growth rates in many coastal cities of the developing world substantially exceed growth rates in surrounding rural regions. Of the world cities with a population of 500,000 or more, nearly 40 percent are located on the shore.[23] (See figure.)

The United States is a maritime state, relying on the guaranteed use of the seas for both its economic well-being and its

World cities at night.

ability to project military power in support of its national interests. For any global power, seapower is essential. Even with extensive strategic airlift capability, the sea remains the only viable means to move and sustain sizable military forces. As the number of U.S. bases overseas has decreased in the last years of the twentieth century, the importance of forward-deployed U.S. naval power, with its amphibious capability for forcible entry, has increased dramatically.

The worldwide proliferation of weapons and munitions, including chemical and biological munitions will make the security of expeditionary forces against terrorist acts or other attacks a significant issue. Land-based expeditionary forces and their support will be continually at risk. Adding security forces for protection will paradoxically increase the potential targets for terrorist attack and may also increase the likelihood of undesired political friction and incident. In many parts of the developing world, contagious diseases may pose an additional threat to expeditionary forces ashore. Finally, situations may arise in which the host nation does not desire a large U.S. presence ashore. The sea is thus becoming increasingly important militarily not only as a vital means for moving military forces but as a secure base of operations, not merely for initially projecting power ashore but for the duration of the expeditionary operation. In the future, an important factor may be the ability to conduct and sustain expeditionary operations from sea bases.

As the range at which naval forces can project power inland increases, an increasingly larger portion of the globe falls under the potential influence of U.S. naval power. Just as it is undeniable that there is no alternative to the sea for world trade, it is equally undeniable that there is no alternative to naval power for the global projection of military influence.

WEAPONRY

Trends in weapons distribution pose two main areas of concern. The first is the proliferation of weapons of mass destruction—nuclear, chemical, and biological weapons. Although obviously dangerous, nuclear weapons are possessed by relatively few of our potential enemies because of their expense and technical complexity. Nonetheless, while the number of admitted, confirmed, or suspected nuclear powers remains relatively small, several of them are hostile to the United States.[24] Moreover, the technical knowledge required to produce nuclear weapons is spreading. Especially with the dissolution of the Soviet Union and the dispersal of its nuclear arsenal, it becomes more likely that the possession of these weapons will not be limited to established, responsible states.

Chemical weapons are more widespread than nuclear weapons, and their availability already extends beyond established governments to other political groups, as demonstrated by the attack by the cult Aum Shinri Kyo in Japan in 1995. Twelve people were killed and more than 5,000 injured by the release of the nerve agent sarin on the Tokyo subway during rush hour. The "poor man's nuclear weapon," chemical weapons offer significant destructive effect at a relatively low cost. Regardless of treaties, it is difficult to regulate the development and stockpiling of such weapons. As with chemical weapons, the development of a biological weapons capability by a potentially hostile political group is difficult to detect and prevent.

The targets of weapons of mass destruction are not necessarily military ones. Terrorist organizations are just as likely to use these weapons against civilian populations. Furthermore, weapons of mass destruction do not necessarily require an advanced delivery system such as a missile or aircraft; an automobile, a suitcase, or even a small glass vial could suffice. The proliferation of weapons of mass destruction is perhaps the gravest single threat to national security in the short term.

The other trend of concern is the increasing availability of inexpensive but lethal conventional weapons ranging from mines to rocket grenades to car bombs to shoulder-launched antiaircraft missiles. These weapons are extremely effective, portable, highly destructive, easy to operate, difficult to detect and counteract, practically impossible to regulate, and in need of little technical or logistical support. These weapons can often be manufactured locally or are readily available on the international arms market. They are abundant and pose a significant threat to military and civilian targets alike. When in the hands of terrorists or other nonstate actors, this threat is particularly difficult to counter. Even in the poorest regions of the world, these weapons will likely be widespread.

CONCLUSION

While arguably threats to national security have decreased in magnitude, they have increased in number, frequency, and variety. Far from creating a period of global peace, the end of the Cold War has ushered in a period of crises and conflicts. We see established nation-states all across the globe splintering along ethnic, religious, or tribal lines. These trends not only produce crises between and within nations but create a much greater degree of instability—instability that can eventually degenerate into chaos. Where crises rise from relatively stable states led by state actors (premiers or presidents), chaos is the by-product of growing change and uncertainty, and is typically led by non-state actors (tribal chiefs and warlords). In this chaotic world, the United States will have to respond in defense of national interests. Many, perhaps even most, of these crises will occur in the heavily populated littoral regions of the developing world. As a result, the protection of national interests requires a strong, responsive naval expeditionary capability. That is the subject of chapter 2.

Chapter 2

The Nature of Expeditionary Operations

"Since men live upon the land and not upon the sea, great issues between nations at war have always been decided—except in the rarest cases—either by what your army can do against your enemy's territory and national life or else by the fear of what the fleet makes it possible for your army to do."[1]

—Julian S. Corbett

"Word came on May 27 that another revolution was in full swing at Bluefields, on the east coast of Nicaragua. We received orders to leave at eight thirty in the morning and by eleven thirty were on our way—two hundred and fifty officers and men. Mrs. Butler had [gone] . . . to do some shopping. When she returned at noon, I was gone . . . ."[2]

—Smedley D. Butler

B ased on the wide variety of overseas crises and conflicts described in chapter 1, this chapter discusses the nature and requirements of expeditionary operations and the Marine Corps' role in and approach to their conduct.

NATIONAL INTERESTS, CRISIS PREVENTION, AND CRISIS RESPONSE

Chapter 1 described a chaotic world where threats to U.S. interests may arise quickly and in unexpected places. The national security strategy places these interests into three categories: vital interests of broad, overriding importance to the survival, safety, and vitality of the United States; important interests that affect national well-being; and humanitarian interests.[3]

History teaches that our nation's interests are less likely to be threatened when other nations are at peace, and their political, economic, and social systems are relatively stable. Therefore, peacetime deterrence is one of the military's most important roles in shaping the international environment. A capable military and the resolve to use it against a potential adversary are key to effective deterrence. By preventing a potential belligerent from taking actions that threaten the interests of the United States or our allies, the military helps promote regional stability and fosters an environment where differences and issues can be resolved or addressed peacefully.

Even with the best efforts at deterrence, complex and chaotic conditions in the world will inevitably produce crisis and conflict. Therefore, protection of the interests of the United States and its allies demands an effective crisis-response capability—the ability to respond quickly and effectively to a wide variety of potentially dangerous situations. Not all crises require a military response. However, when diplomatic, economic, and informational power prove inadequate, the ability to apply military power is essential to the protection of national interests. Military action may not be the preferred solution, and it may be used infrequently, but under some conditions the United States will inevitably find it necessary to use military force.

An effective military response to an overseas crisis involving U.S. interests often requires the expeditionary capability to intervene or interpose in foreign political controversies. A military intervention is the deliberate act of a nation or group of nations to introduce its military forces into the course of an existing controversy in order to influence events. A military interposition, on the other hand, is the deliberate act of a nation to introduce military forces into a foreign country during a crisis to protect its citizens from harm without otherwise becoming involved in the course of the crisis. The ability to act swiftly in such circumstances may be the best way to contain, resolve, or mitigate the consequences of a crisis that could otherwise become more costly and deadly.

Crisis response requires the full spectrum of military capabilities, including the capability for forcible entry—the introduction of military forces in the face of organized, armed resistance. National interest requires an expeditionary crisis-response force specifically organized, trained, equipped, and deployed to project military power overseas. Because of the unpredictability of potential crises, such crisis-response forces should be designed with a broad range of capabilities rather than in response to a specific threat. Such a rapid-response, general-purpose force must maintain itself in a continuous state of readiness, ready to deploy rapidly by both air and sea and able to adapt to a broad range of operating environments on short notice.

EXPEDITIONARY OPERATIONS DEFINED AND DISCUSSED

An expedition is a military operation conducted by an armed force to accomplish a specific objective in a foreign country.[4] The missions of military expeditions may vary widely. Examples of missions of military expeditions include providing humanitarian assistance in times of disaster or disruption;

establishing and keeping peace in a foreign country; protecting U.S. citizens or commerce abroad; retaliating for an act of aggression by a foreign political group; and destroying an enemy government by defeating its armed forces in combat.

The defining characteristic of expeditionary operations is the projection of force into a foreign setting.[5] By definition, an expedition thus involves the deployment of military forces to the scene of the crisis or conflict and their requisite support some significant distance from their home bases. These forces may already have been forward-deployed, as in the case of a Marine expeditionary unit (special operations capable), deployed aboard Navy amphibious ships and ready for immediate employment, or they may be required to deploy from their home bases in response to a developing situation. Expeditionary operations involve the establishment of forward bases, land or sea, from which military power can be brought to bear on the situation. An expeditionary operation thus requires the temporary creation of a support apparatus necessary to sustain the operation to its conclusion. Logistics, the movement and maintenance of forces—the "mounting" of the expedition—is thus a central consideration in the conduct of expeditionary operations.[6]

In some cases an expeditionary force may accomplish its mission without the direct application of coercive force by merely establishing a visible and credible presence nearby. However, this indirect influence can result only from the perception of a nation's capability and willingness to physically establish military forces on foreign soil if necessary, and so the ability to project a physical presence remains central. Furthermore, in some situations presence must be established in the face of hostile resistance—that is, through forcible entry.

All expeditions involve the projection of power into a foreign setting. However, it is important to recognize that not all power projection constitutes expeditionary operations; power projection is a necessary component but not a sufficient condition by itself to constitute an expeditionary operation. Operations that do not involve actual deployment of forces are not expeditionary operations.

Power projection does not imply that expeditionary operations are by definition offensive. The initial deployment of forces to the Persian Gulf in 1990, Operation Desert Shield, had the mission of defending Saudi Arabia against an Iraqi attack. Only when the defense of Saudi Arabia was secured did Desert Shield give way to preparations for Desert Storm, the offensive to liberate Kuwait. Desert Storm in turn gave way to Operation Provide Comfort, a humanitarian mission to protect Kurds against Iraqi attacks and to provide food, water, and shelter for thousands of Kurdish refugees along the Turkish border.

An expeditionary force need not be primarily a ground combat organization. Even in humanitarian operations, an expeditionary force will invariably include some ground forces, if only to provide local security. However, the composition of an expeditionary force depends on the requirements of the mission. For example, an expeditionary force may consist of aviation units to operate and fly missions out of an expeditionary airfield, supported by only a small security force. In disaster relief or refugee control missions, the predominant forces may be combat service support.

Expeditionary forces vary significantly in size and composition. The American Expeditionary Force, for example, that fought in the First World War eventually totaled some two million troops in 42 infantry divisions plus supporting organizations. The special purpose MAGTF that conducted Operation Eastern Exit, the evacuation of the U.S. Embassy in Mogadishu, Somalia, in 1991, consisted of a reinforced helicopter squadron, a combat service support detachment, and less than one battalion of infantry embarked on two amphibious ships.

Expeditionary operations may also vary greatly in scope, ranging from full-scale combat to noncombat missions. Operation Desert Storm was an overwhelming offensive to defeat Iraqi forces by offensive air and mechanized ground operations following a massive, deliberate buildup of forces and supplies. Operation Assured Response in April 1996 was much more limited, consisting of the evacuation by the 22d Marine Expeditionary Unit (special operations capable) of more than 2,100 people from Liberia in the face of sporadic violence.

The term "expeditionary" implies a temporary duration with the intention to withdraw from foreign soil after the accomplishment of the specified mission. The American Expeditionary Force first helped repulse German offensives in France in the spring of 1918 and then participated in continuous combat until the end of the war in November, at which point it returned home. In contrast, Operation Eastern Exit, the evacuation of the U.S. embassy in Somalia in 1991, was of much shorter duration. From the time the U.S. Ambassador requested military assistance to the time the evacuees were offloaded in Oman, the expedition lasted 10 days, although the actual evacuation operation, from the launching of the first wave of helicopters to the return of the last wave with the withdrawing security force, lasted only 24 hours. An operation that involves a permanent or indefinite presence supported by a standing organization and infrastructure such as the U.S. forces stationed in Europe, Japan, or Korea ceases to be an expedition and becomes a permanent station.

The term "expeditionary" also implies austere conditions and support. This does not mean that an expeditionary force is necessarily small or lightly equipped, but that it is no larger or heavier than necessary to accomplish the mission. Supplies, equipment, and infrastructure are limited to operational necessities; amenities are strictly minimized. Expeditionary bases or airfields, for example, provide less than the full range of support typically associated with permanent stations. Operational considerations such as force protection and intelligence prevail over administrative, quality-of-life, or other considerations. This tendency toward austerity derives from security

considerations, the temporary nature of expeditionary operations, and the imperative to minimize lift and support
requirements.

In summary, to perform expeditionary operations requires a
special mindset—one that is constantly prepared for immediate
deployment overseas into austere operating environments,
bringing everything necessary to accomplish the mission. There
are different ways to conduct expeditionary operations, and the
various armed Services provide differing but complementary
capabilities. In general, naval expeditionary forces provide a
self-sustaining, sea-based capability for immediate or rapid response, especially through forward deployment. Land-based
forces, on the other hand, generally require a longer deployment phase and the creation of an in-theater logistics apparatus
to achieve the buildup of decisive force. While all the Services
include units capable of expeditionary operations, the entire
operating forces of the Marine Corps are specifically organized, equipped, and train- ed for expeditionary service.

REASONS FOR CONDUCTING EXPEDITIONARY OPERATIONS

Some political objectives can be secured through the actual or
potential destruction that long-range bombing or the precision
fires of a fleet can provide. Some potential aggressors can be
deterred and some actual aggressors can be compelled to

change their behavior through the threat of punishment from afar. That said, there are many policy aims or military missions that can be accomplished only by establishing a potent military force on foreign soil. In numerous situations, physical destruction alone cannot achieve policy aims, or massive destruction is inconsistent with political goals. Because, as Corbett's epigraph at the beginning of this chapter suggests, political issues are ultimately decided on land, there will be no shortage of conflicts requiring an ongoing physical presence at the scene of the conflict. Expeditionary operations will thus be required for a variety of reasons, including—

- To assure that policy objectives pursued by other means have in fact been secured; for example, to ensure compliance with established diplomatic solutions such as the adherence to cease-fire arrangements or an agreement to hold free elections.

- To seize or control key physical objectives such as airports, ports, resource areas, or political centers in order to ensure their safe use by all groups, to deny their use to an enemy or disruptive element, or to facilitate future actions such as the introduction of follow-on forces.

- To control urban or other restrictive terrain.

- To establish a close, physical, and highly visible presence in order to demonstrate political resolve, deter aggressive action, or compel desired behavior.

- To establish and maintain order in an area beset by chaos and disorder.

- To protect or rescue U.S. citizens or other civilians.

- To separate warring groups from each other or from the population at large, especially when enemy or disruptive elements are embedded in the population.

- To provide physical relief and assistance in the event of disaster.[7]

SEQUENCE IN PROJECTING EXPEDITIONARY FORCES

The projection of an expeditionary force generally occurs in the following sequence:

- Predeployment actions.
- Deployment.
- Entry.
- Enabling actions.
- Decisive actions.
- Redeployment.

This sequence is in no way meant to dictate the phases of an operation. It merely provides a framework for discussion and further understanding.

All military expeditions begin with planning and predeployment actions. These actions include the commander's organization of the deployment to ensure that forces arrive in the objective area in a logical sequence, at the right time, and with the correct equipment and sustainment to support the concept of operation.

Deployment is the movement of forces, their equipment, and their sustainment to either a theater of operations or an objective area in accordance with the commander's plan. Airlift is normally the quickest way to deploy forces, although it requires the presence of a secure airhead at the destination. The quickest way to introduce significant, sustainable forces is by sealift. Maritime prepositioning force operations, discussed in chapter 4, combine the advantages of both airlift and sealift. The initial U.S. forces deploying to Operation Desert Shield, including the 7th and 1st Marine Expeditionary Brigades,[8] arrived by air, although the equipment and supplies for the Marine brigades arrived aboard maritime prepositioning ships. In the end, 90 percent of U.S. forces and supplies arrived by sea.

The speed at which capable forces can be deployed to the scene of a crisis is often vitally important. The more quickly forces can deploy to stabilize a situation, the greater will be the likelihood of eventual success and the less may be the eventual

cost. What matters, however, is not just how quickly the first
forces can deploy; it is the speed at which capable, sustainable
forces can deploy. Thus, an expeditionary force deploys by
phases in support of the commander's concept of operations.
Typically, forward-deployed or rapidly deployable forces move
as the initial crisis response, followed by other, often heavier
forces deploying more slowly. The Marine Corps achieves
rapid deployment through placing some forces in ships and
other locations abroad, through transporting some forces by
air, and through placing some supplies in ships and other locations abroad.

It is not enough to be able to deploy forces to a foreign theater. There is also the problem of access, gained by force if necessary. Many expeditionary forces are not capable of forcible
entry, although all amphibious forces are. "Entry" refers to the
initial introduction of forces onto foreign soil. During this period, expeditionary forces are often at greatest risk, and for this
reason, the introduction of forces is often a complicated military evolution. Entry is normally accomplished by seaborne or
airborne movement, although in some cases forces may be in-
troduced by ground movement from an expeditionary base in
an adjacent country. Historically, entry has required the establishment of an expeditionary base ashore from which to operate, but this is not necessary if the expeditionary force can
operate effectively from a sea base. Key to the entry phase is
the presence or creation of some entry point—an available airfield or port, an assailable coast line, a suitable and support-
able drop zone, or an accessible frontier. The most difficult

type of entry is forcible entry—seizing a lodgment area in hostile territory via combat. Not all expeditionary operations involve forcible entry. Many involve the introduction of forces into a permissive environment or an environment that has not yet turned hostile. Because there is always a potential for hostile resistance and because the level of hostility can change quickly, a forcible-entry capability is a permanent requirement for successful expeditionary opera- tions.

Enabling actions refer to those preparatory actions taken by the expeditionary force to facilitate the eventual accomplishment of the mission. Deployment and entry could also be thought of as enabling actions, but because of their importance and particular requirements, we have considered them separately. With the possible exception of expeditions of very limited scope and duration, such as a noncombatant evacuation or a punitive raid, the forces that can initially deploy and enter an area will rarely be sufficient to accomplish the mission. Usually, other forces will follow, and the initial forces will undertake actions that are designed to set the stage for the eventual decisive actions. Enabling actions may include, for example, seizing a port or airfield to facilitate the secure introduction of follow-on forces. They may include establishing the necessary logistics and other support capabilities. In cases of disaster or disruption, enabling actions usually involve the initial restoration of order or stability. In the case of open warfare, enabling actions may involve operations to seize a lodgment area for follow-on forces or to capture key terrain necessary for the conduct of decisive operations.

Decisive actions are those actions intended to create the conditions that will accomplish the political objective—in other words, to accomplish the mission. In disasters, they include relief operations. In disruptions, they often include peacemaking and peacekeeping until local governmental control can be reestablished. In conflict, they usually involve the military defeat of the enemy's fighting forces. In Operation Desert Shield, for example, the decisive actions were those undertaken to protect Saudi Arabia against Iraqi attack. In Operation Desert Storm, the decisive actions were the offensive to eject Iraqi forces from Kuwait and destroy their offensive capability. In Operation Provide Comfort, the decisive actions were those to protect the Kurds from Iraqi attack and to provide humanitarian aid. In Operation Restore Democracy, the 1994–1995 intervention in Haiti, the decisive actions were those to restore and support the democratically elected government and to ensure the peaceful transition of authority through the next election.

Because expeditions are by definition temporary, all expeditionary operations involve a redeployment—the departure of the expeditionary force or a transition to a permanent presence of some sort. This is often one of the most difficult aspects of expeditionary operations. An "exit strategy" therefore must be an important consideration in both the initial decision to take military action and the conduct of operations. Departure is not as simple as the tactical withdrawal of the expeditionary force from the scene. It requires the withdrawing of force in a way that maintains the desired political situation. If a situation has been stabilized to the point that the local government can maintain peaceful order, military forces may depart altogether. It is more likely, however, that the expeditionary force will be replaced by a longer-lasting presence, whether an occupation force, an observation force, or some nonmilitary agency. For example, Operation Provide Comfort, the relief effort that was initially conducted primarily by military forces previously deployed for Desert Storm, was turned over to the United Nations High Commission on Refugees in June 1991. At that point, military forces, including the 24th Marine Expeditionary Unit (Special Operations Capable), began departing northern Iraq.

Although a similar sequence of phases can be seen in many expeditionary operations, they are conducted in many different ways. What follows is a discussion of the Marine Corps' approach to the conduct of expeditionary operations.

EXPEDITIONARY MINDSET

The most important element in the Marine Corps' conduct of expeditionary operations is not a particular organization, family of equipment, or tactic. It is a state of mind. For the Marine Corps, being "expeditionary" is, before anything else, a mindset. The epigraph by Smedley Butler at the beginning of this chapter captures this attitude. Just as every Marine is a rifleman regardless of duties and military specialty, all Marines must also think of themselves as part of a fundamentally expeditionary organization designed and intended to project military force overseas. This expeditionary mindset is epitomized by the phrase "bags packed"—that is, ready and willing to deploy on a moment's notice, any time, to any place, to perform any mission. All operating forces, rather than selected ready units, must maintain themselves in a high state of deployability and general readiness. The expeditionary mindset implies a Spartan attitude: an expectation and a willingness to endure—in fact, a certain pride in enduring—hardship and austere conditions. As an example of this attitude, embarkation boxes substitute for bookcases, even in garrison, and creature comforts are minimal.

An expeditionary mindset implies the versatility and adaptability to respond effectively without a great deal of preparation time to a broad variety of circumstances. Another part of this expeditionary mindset is a global perspective oriented to responding to a diverse range of threats around the globe rather than to a specific threat in a specific part of the world.

This mindset is a matter of training and institutional culture. Commanders must realize the continuous importance of imparting and maintaining this attitude within their units.

NAVAL CHARACTER

The Marine Corps is fundamentally a naval service. Marines are "soldiers of the sea," trained to operate on the sea but to fight on the land. This distinction is more than just historical or cultural—although it is that also. It is first a matter of practical significance. The sea remains the only viable way to deploy large military forces to distant theaters and to rapidly shift forces between theaters. Additionally, in many situations, sea basing provides a viable, secure option for sustaining expeditionary operations. Given the range of naval aviation, few parts of the globe are beyond the operational reach of naval expeditionary forces today. For a country that possesses naval dominance, the sea becomes an avenue for projecting military power practically anywhere in the world.

The Marine Corps' naval character facilitates global sourcing, the composition of an expeditionary force by Marine elements from anywhere in the world. I Marine Expeditionary Force in Operation Desert Storm was composed of forces from bases on the U.S.'s east and west coasts and in the Pacific. Naval mobility similarly facilitates the rapid and flexible shifting of forces between theaters.

There is more to naval expeditionary power projection, however, than using the sea to provide strategic or operational mobility. There is also the significant practical problem of projecting military power from the sea onto land in the face of hostile resistance. In the words of General George C. Marshall: "A landing against organized and highly trained opposition is probably the most difficult undertaking which military forces are called upon to face."[9] Amphibious operations require a high degree of training to achieve proficiency. All Marine Corps forces are specifically organized, trained, and equipped to deploy aboard, operate from, and sustain themselves from Navy ships. They are specifically designed to project land combat power ashore from the sea. Forcible entry through amphibious landing remains the Marine Corps' specialty.[10] Given a decreasing permanent U.S. military presence overseas and the volatility in the littoral regions of the developing world, this amphibious expertise provided by the Marine Corps is one of the most valuable components in the Nation's power projection capabilities.

STRATEGIC MOBILITY: CLOSURE RATE AND GLOBAL REACH

In an age of global uncertainty and rapidly developing crises, closure rate and global reach are critical expeditionary considerations. Closure rate refers to how quickly a military force can close on an objective area once tasked. The ability to close quickly is extremely important, especially in the early stages of a developing situation. Reach refers to the geographical limits to which a force can deploy and sustain credible military power. Both considerations are functions of strategic mobility, the capability to deploy and sustain military forces worldwide in support of national strategy.[11]

In large part, although not exclusively, the Marine Corps gains its strategic mobility from its naval character. Marine Corps forces maintain strategic mobility in three ways. First is through the forward deployment of combined arms, general-purpose operating forces in the form of Marine air-ground task forces (MAGTFs). The composition and capabilities of MAGTFs are discussed in chapter 3. Deployed aboard amphibious Navy ships, these task forces maintain a continuous presence at strategic locations around the globe and can be rapidly moved to and indefinitely stationed at the scene of potential trouble. Because the globe is dominated by water, there are few locations beyond the reach of forward-deployed MAGTFs. When deploying to an objective area, naval forces can move continuously, unlike land or air forces, which must suspend movement for rest and replenishment. Also unlike land or air forces, naval forces can loiter indefinitely near the scene of a potential crisis. A good example of this ability to loiter is Operation Sharp Edge, the evacuation of Liberia in 1990. Amphibious Squadron 4 and the 22d Marine Expeditionary Unit (special operations capable) arrived off the coast of Liberia on 3 June 1990 as the situation in that country deteriorated. They remained on station, some 50 miles offshore, for 62 days before evacuation operations were required starting 5 August.

The second element of Marine Corps strategic mobility is the prepositioning of equipment and supplies aboard ships at sea. The advantage of maritime prepositioning is that Marines can link up in an objective area with prepositioned equipment and supplies more quickly than those same Marines can deploy from their home base with their equipment and supplies. As with forward-deployed MAGTFs, prepositioned equipment and supplies can be moved quickly nearly anywhere in the world and can be maintained indefinitely near the scene of a potential crisis. Chapter 3 discusses the organization of maritime prepositioning forces while chapter 4 discusses maritime prepositioning force operations.

The third element of Marine Corps strategic mobility is the rapid deployability of units by sea and air. Strategic airlift is generally the faster way to deploy but is limited in the amount of lift. Strategic airlift also requires a secure airhead for the introduction of forces, whereas naval amphibious shipping can support forcible entry. Shipping generally cannot match airlift for speed of deployment but remains the only viable means for deploying large forces and adequate supplies and equipment. All Marine Corps operating forces are specifically organized and equipped for deployment aboard Navy amphibious ships.

OPERATIONAL MOBILITY

Operational mobility is the capability of military forces to move from place to place within a theater to perform their missions. Whereas strategic mobility is the ability to move from theater to theater and tactical mobility is the ability to move in combat, operational mobility is the ability to move between engagements or other actions within the context of the campaign. Operational mobility is a function of range and sustained speed over a significant distance. The Marine Corps achieves operational mobility in several ways: through amphibious shipping, assault support aircraft, landing craft, assault amphibious vehicles, and light armored vehicles.

Although we typically think of shipping as a component of strategic mobility, it may also be employed to significant operational effect as well. In many cases, a MAGTF carried on amphibious shipping can enjoy greater operational mobility along a coastline than an enemy moving along the coast by land. This is especially true when the naval force has the ability to interfere with an enemy's use of roads. This may likewise be true in the developing world where road systems may not be adequate for the movement of large, mechanized formations. In this way, the sea can be an avenue of approach rather than an obstacle to movement, and the amphibious force maneuvers by landing at the time and place of its own choosing, where the enemy is vulnerable. An excellent example of this is Operation Chromite, MacArthur's landing of the 1st Marine Division at Inchon in September 1950 to dramatically sever North Korean lines of communications during the Korean War.

OPERATIONAL AND TACTICAL COMPETENCE

Operational and tactical competence refers to the consistent ability of the organization to effectively accomplish assigned missions and tasks. More simply, competence is the ability to "get things done," and it is obviously an essential element of effective expeditionary operations. Competence is a broad and largely intangible quality based on, among other factors, experience, doctrine, technical proficiency, training, education, and leadership.

Experience is perhaps the single most important factor in developing operational and tactical competence. Experience provides understanding of the practical problems of execution and an appreciation for what is feasible and what is not. Doctrine contributes the body of concepts and principles that guide action. The Marine Corps' institutional doctrinal philosophy is based on tempo, surprise, and focused exploitation of enemy critical vulnerabilities, a doctrine called maneuver warfare.

One of the purposes of training and education is to instill sound judgment in leaders at all levels. Competence requires leaders who can see beyond the tactical requirements of the immediate problem and who understand the larger impli-cations of their decisions—to include the nature of military action as an element of politics and policy. Technical proficiency refers to expertise in the employment of equipment and procedures and is largely a function of individual and unit training. Marine leadership is best summarized by the principle of leadership by example. Finally, competence requires capable, reliable equipment and support, which is not to say that it always requires the most advanced equipment avail- able.

Competence is a complex combination of various skills and qualities. Furthermore, competence is situationally dependent. What it takes to be competent with respect to one mission may not be what it takes to be competent with respect to another mission.

SUSTAINABILITY

Effective expeditionary operations are not merely a matter of projecting military power but also of sustaining that power throughout the duration of the expedition. Sustainability is the ability to maintain the necessary level and duration of operational activity to achieve military objectives. It is a function of providing for and maintaining the levels of forces, matériel, and supplies needed to support military effort.[12] Sustainability can be an especially important consideration in the developing world, where many regions often lack the infrastructure necessary to support highly advanced military forces.

Expeditionary operations generally involve the establishment of some forward operating base or bases near the scene of the action. This may be an expeditionary land or sea base or a combination of both. Sea bases have the advantage of being ready-made and ready-to-operate when a naval expeditionary force deploys, whereas land bases must be established ashore. Sea bases also have the advantage of being easily retrievable at the end of the operation, facilitating departure and redeployment. However, sea bases are limited by shipping capacity, technical challenges of offloading and ship-to-shore movement, and the access limitations imposed by combat loading requirements. The last two of these are partially offset by efficient procedures developed over time by the Navy and Marine Corps as the result of extensive experience. The limits of sea bases will be further offset as new ship designs facilitate accessibility of supplies and selective offloading. The relative security of expeditionary land and sea bases is situation-dependent, based on the capabilities of the enemy. In many cases, sea bases are more secure, especially in situations in which friendly naval forces dominate the seas. However, in some cases, expeditionary bases may actually be more secure, as in the Falklands War of 1982 in which the greatest British losses were ships sunk by Argentine air-to-surface missiles. This said, the conditions likely to prevail in future expeditionary operations—threats of disease and rear area attack, host-nation sensitivity to a large foreign presence—argue for an increase in the importance and utility of sea basing. Effectiveness in future expeditionary operations will require the ability to operate routinely and continuously from sea bases.

A self-contained sustainment capability can be an important logistic consideration in expeditionary operations, especially in the early stages of deployment before a theater sustainment system has been put in place. All MAGTFs deploy with the supplies necessary to sustain the force until reinforcements arrive.

Finally, another important consideration for sustaining an expeditionary force is the support requirements of the force. A military force able to operate under the most austere conditions can be at a significant advantage, especially in undeveloped regions that lack the infrastructure to satisfy massive logistic requirements. Such a force is more easily sustained and is less adversely affected by logistic limitations. It places less of a demand on strategic, operational, and tactical lift. It requires a smaller expeditionary base, which enhances force protection. Because expeditionary operations are by definition temporary, a smaller, lighter footprint simplifies the problems of redeployment.

ADAPTABILITY

Adaptability is the capacity to change—tactics, techniques, organizations, and so on—in anticipation of or in response to changes in the situation. In an uncertain, chaotic world environment, adaptability is an essential characteristic of effective expeditionary operations. The more quickly an organization can adapt in a changing environment, the more effective it will be.

53

We can adapt through improvisation, departing from the planned action in response to an unexpected change in the situation. At the lowest echelons, where decision cycles are short, improvisation may involve a truly spontaneous action. At higher echelons, where decision cycles are likely to be longer, improvisation is more likely to involve rapid modification of the existing plan. In any event, improvisation involves a specific, untested response to a particular set of unexpected conditions.

We can also adapt through innovation, the systematic adoption of new operating methods, organizations, or technologies either in response to actual experience or in anticipation of likely need. An improvisation that proves to have general value can become an innovation through its systematic adoption and refinement. In fact, this is a common source of innovation. A good example of innovation is the Marine Corps' development of amphibious warfare doctrine, methods, and equipment after the First World War in anticipation of war in the Pacific against Japan. Innovation should not be the result only of formal programs but should also "bubble up" from the bottom of the organization as operating units down to the lowest levels develop, institutionalize, and pass on valuable new methods. Commanders at all levels must not only be open to innovation but must actively encourage it from subordinates. Only by these complementary top-down and bottom-up processes of innovation can the Marine Corps maintain the necessary adaptiveness.

As with most of the other characteristics of effective expeditionary operations, adaptability is largely a function of mindset. It requires leaders at all levels with flexibility of mind who are willing to exercise judgment and initiative on the basis of situational awareness rather than merely to follow orders and apply techniques by rote. This ability is largely a function of training, education, and especially institutional culture. Adaptability requires a learning organization—an organization that is self-critical and is able to change quickly in response to its experiences.

Adaptability also has an important organizational aspect. Balanced, multidimensional, general-purpose organizations demonstrate adaptability through the ability to task-organize rapidly and effectively on the basis of the requirements of each situation.

Adaptability has a doctrinal aspect as well. The maneuver warfare concept of mission tactics requires leaders down to the lowest levels to exercise local initiative on the basis of their understanding of the larger situation and intent. This decentralized form of command and control increases the speed at which an organization can adapt to changing situations.

RECONSTITUTION

Reconstitution refers to the ability of an expeditionary force to regenerate, reorganize, replenish, and reorient itself for a new mission after employment elsewhere without having to return to home base. This is not merely the ability to divert from an original deployment to another mission but to complete one mission ashore and then redeploy to perform another. It is the ability to project expeditionary power anew from an existing expeditionary base or forward-deployed status. The ability to reconstitute is a source of the adaptability that is vitally important in modern expeditionary operations. It can save significant time and cost in deploying to meet an emerging crisis. For example, in October 1983, the 22d Marine Amphibious Unit was diverted to Grenada while en route to Lebanon. The Marine amphibious unit conducted landings as part of Operation Urgent Fury at Grenada on 25 October and at Carriacou on 1 November. By 3 November, the Marine amphibious unit was reembarked aboard its amphibious shipping and had resumed its passage to Lebanon. Another example is the 5th Marine Expeditionary Brigade's participation in Operation Sea Angel in April 1991. The brigade was returning home via the Indian Ocean from duty during Operation Desert Storm when it was diverted to Bangladesh to provide disaster relief in the wake of a cyclone that had left millions homeless.

The Marine Corps' ability to reconstitute combat power comes from several sources. First is the nature of the MAGTF as a combined arms, general-purpose force readily tailorable to different situations. MAGTFs are readily and routinely reorganized during both deployment and employment. This allows a MAGTF performing one mission to reorganize quickly for another. Second is the naval character of Marine forces and the self-contained nature of MAGTFs deployed aboard amphibious ships. Self-contained, sea-based sustainment allows Marine expeditionary forces to be reemployed without the need to first put in place a sustainment system. The existing system for sustaining routinely forward-deployed units can also be used to reconstitute combat power.

COST-EFFECTIVENESS

It is difficult to put a price on national security or to weigh the cost of action versus inaction in any particular crisis. When costs and benefits are measured in terms of human life, traditional cost-benefit analysis becomes inadequate. However, the resources of the United States are not unlimited. Consequently, it is imperative as a general principle that military forces conduct expeditions as economically as possible. The need for economy becomes especially important in an uncertain era characterized by unexpected crises requiring the unanticipated and unbudgeted allocation of military force.

Cost-effectiveness does not simply mean accomplishing a mission inexpensively. Too small a commitment early may lead at best to an unnecessarily larger commitment later and at worst to a failed mission. As with the military principle of economy of force, cost-effectiveness here means accom- plishing the mission with no greater cost or commitment than is necessary to accomplish the mission properly.

Several factors contribute to cost-effectiveness. First, the Marine Corps routinely forward-deploys expeditionary forces and equipment near the scene of potential crises. This cuts down on the cost of deployment in response to an operational need because much of the cost of deployment is covered in routine operating expenses. The regenerative ability described earlier contributes to this aspect of cost-effectiveness. Additionally, routine deployments with the Navy develop institutional proficiency and efficiency at deploying. The requirements of being routinely deployed aboard ship imbue the institutional culture with a decidedly Spartan character.

Versatility is another source of cost-effectiveness—for example, the ability to task-organize for a wide variety of contingencies. This versatility applies to equipment as well. The assault amphibious vehicles and helicopters, for example, that provide mobility from ship to objective in amphibious operations also provide mechanized or helicopterborne tactical mobility during operations ashore and are invaluable in supporting disaster relief operations in the littorals. This kind of versatility can translate into major cost savings by minimizing the requirement for specialized units and equipment.

CONCLUSION

As the sole remaining superpower in an increasingly intercon- nected world, the United States finds its national interests af- fected by events in every part of the globe. These interests include vital interests of national survival, important interests of national well-being, and humanitarian interests. While politi- cal, economic, and psychological components of national power play an important role in responding to worldwide cri- ses, the preservation of the national interest also demands the ability to project military force into foreign countries. The abil- ity to respond quickly and effectively to the entire range of po- litical crises anywhere in the world is the foundation of national military strategy. There will be numerous missions requiring expeditionary operations—sometimes the physical establish- ment of a military force on foreign soil, in the face of hostile resistance. The rest of this publication describes the organiza- tions and concepts with which the Marine Corps provides that capability through the conduct of expeditionary operations.

Chapter 3

Expeditionary Organizations

"Under all circumstances, a decisive naval superiority is to be considered a fundamental principle, and the basis upon which all hope of success must ultimately depend."[1]

—George Washington, 1780

"There's no reason for having a Navy and Marine Corps. General Bradley tells me that amphibious operations are a thing of the past. We'll never have any more amphibious operations. That does away with the Marine Corps. And the Air Force can do anything the Navy can do nowadays, so that does away with the Navy."[2]

—Secretary of Defense Louis A. Johnson, December 1949

M arine Corps forces are organized and equipped specifically to meet the requirements of expeditionary operations. These organizations possess the characteristics of versatility, flexibility, expandability, rapid deployability, sustainability, and reconstitutive ability necessary for expeditionary operations. This chapter describes the way the Marine Corps organizes for such operations.

NAVAL EXPEDITIONARY FORCES

The Navy and Marine Corps provide naval expeditionary forces as part of a joint force. These forces are organized to accomplish a specific objective in a foreign country.[3] They are designed to project military power ashore from the sea, to include the establishment of a landing force on foreign soil if needed, and thus to operate in the littoral regions.

Naval expeditionary forces combine the complementary but distinct capabilities of the Navy and Marine Corps. Through attack aircraft, surface fire support, sea-launched cruise missiles, and special-warfare forces, Navy forces provide the capability to attack targets in the littorals, and they provide the capability to deploy, land, and sustain expeditionary forces ashore. Navy forces contribute the seaward element of naval expeditionary power projection. Marine forces contribute landing forces, the landward extension of naval expeditionary power. Landing forces include not only ground combat forces but also Marine aviation and logistics elements that can operate from expeditionary land as well as sea bases.[4] In addition to projecting landing forces ashore, deployed Marine aviation forces can also strike targets ashore operating from aircraft carriers and amphibious ships.

Naval forces operating in international waters can minimize military and political liabilities. Naval expeditionary forces are self-contained, able to conduct most military operations without external support. Operating from the sea, naval expeditionary forces can maintain a presence in an area almost indefinitely, eliminating the need for ground-based staging and reducing the influence that host nations or other local powers can exert on U.S. policy initiatives. Naval expeditionary forces are unencumbered by the treaties and access agreements that land-based forces require to operate overseas.[5]

Through forward presence and deployability, naval expeditionary forces provide a rapid response to many crises or potential crises. Naval forces are typically the first to arrive at the scene of a crisis. As part of a joint force, they can serve as enabling forces by stabilizing a situation and preparing for follow on operations.

Naval expeditionary forces offer the combatant commander a flexible range of options in the support of national interests, covering peacetime missions, crisis, and conflict. They can offer a visible deterrent presence in full view of potential aggressors or can operate from over the horizon to minimize political provocation or gain operational surprise and security. They can perform missions ranging from humanitarian assistance to forcible entry. They have the flexibility to project power inland to a significant depth at the time and place of their own choosing.

MARINE CORPS FORCES COMMANDS

There are three Marine Corps Forces commands: Marine Corps Forces Atlantic (MARFORLANT), Marine Corps Forces Pacific (MARFORPAC), and Marine Corps Forces Reserve (MARFORRES). Marine Corps Forces commanders are part of the Service or administrative chain of command and are responsible to the Commandant of the Marine Corps for equipping, training, administering, and sustaining their forces. These forces include—

- I Marine Expeditionary Force, based in southern California and Arizona, under Marine Corps Forces Pacific.

- II Marine Expeditionary Force, based in North and South Carolina, under Marine Corps Forces Atlantic.

- III Marine Expeditionary Force, based in Okinawa, mainland Japan, and Hawaii, under Marine Corps Forces Pacific.

65

- 4th Marine Division, 4th Marine Aircraft Wing, and 4th Force Service Support Group, stationed throughout the United States, under Marine Corps Forces Reserve.

The commanders of Marine Corps Forces Atlantic and Pacific provide operating forces to combatant commanders or other operational commanders. In this capacity, the commanders of Marine Corps Forces Atlantic and Pacific provide three types of expeditionary elements: amphibious forces, maritime prepositioning forces, and air contingency forces. They also provide special-purpose units tailored for a specific mission, such as mobile training teams or Special Purpose MAGTF Unitas, the annual military cooperation deployment to South America.

The commanders of Marine Corps Forces Atlantic and Pacific are also Marine Corps Service component commanders. For example, Commander, Marine Corps Forces Pacific is assigned as the Marine Corps component commander for U.S Pacific Command and designated as the Marine Corps component commander for U.S Central Command and U.S. Forces Korea. Commander, Marine Corps Forces Atlantic is assigned as the Marine Corps component commander for U.S. Atlantic Command and designated as the Marine Corps component commander for U.S. European Command and U.S. Southern Command. Componency is further discussed later in this chapter.

The commanders of Marine Corps Forces Atlantic and Pacific retain the titles and responsibilities of commanding generals of Fleet Marine Forces (FMFs) Atlantic and Pacific. Fleet Marine Force commanding generals have the status of type commanders and provide forces to the Commander, U.S. Atlantic Fleet and Commander, U.S. Pacific Fleet.[6] For example, the Commander, Marine Corps Forces Pacific, is also the commanding general of Fleet Marine Forces Pacific, responsible to the Commander, U.S. Pacific Fleet, for providing combat-ready expeditionary forces for service with the operating fleet. (See figure, page 68.) This includes, for example, Marine expeditionary units deployed with amphibious ready groups.

The Marine Corps Reserve is closely integrated with the active duty Marine Corps Forces. Within the Service chain of command, the commander of Marine Corps Forces Reserve provides Selected Marine Corps Reserve units and individual augmentees to the active duty Marine Forces when directed by the National Command Authorities through the Commandant of the Marine Corps. The Commander in Chief, U.S. Atlantic Command has training and readiness oversight authority over assigned Selected Marine Corps Reserve units on a continuous basis. He executes his training and readiness oversight authority through Commander, Marine Corps Forces Atlantic. When Selected Marine Corps Reserve units are mobilized or ordered to active duty (other than for training), Commander in Chief, U.S. Atlantic Command exercises combatant command (command authority) and is the force provider to the supported combatant commanders.

```
                    ┌─────────────────┐
                    │   Joint Force   │
                    └─────────────────┘

        ┌─────────────────────────────────────────────┐
        │        ┌──────────────┐   ┌──────────────┐   │
        │        │  Air Force   │   │     Navy     │   │
        │        │  component   │   │  component   │   │
        │        └──────────────┘   └──────────────┘   │
        │                           ┌──────────────┐   │
        │                           │ Fleet Marine │   │
        │                           │  Forces*     │   │
        │                           └──────────────┘   │
┌──────────────┐  ┌──────────────┐         ┌──────────────┐
│    Army      │  │ Marine Corps │         │ Special Ops  │
│  component   │  │ component*   │         │  component   │
└──────────────┘  └──────────────┘         └──────────────┘
```

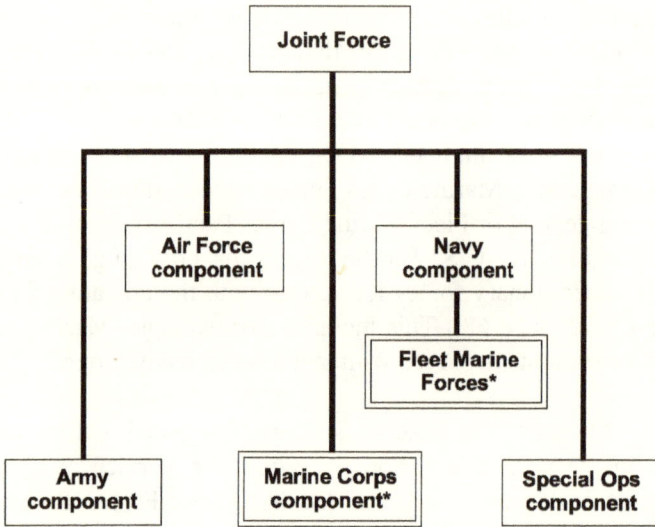

* A Marine Corps Forces commander (COMMARFORLANT or COMMARFORPAC) is designated simultaneously as a Marine Corps component commander (in relation to the joint force commander) and as the commanding general of Fleet Marine Forces (in relation to the Navy component).

The Marine Corps component and the Fleet Marine Forces of a joint force.

MARINE AIR-GROUND TASK FORCES

The MAGTF is the Marine Corps' principal organization for all missions across the range of military operations. The MAGTF provides a combatant commander in chief or other operational commander with a versatile expeditionary force for responding to a broad range of crisis and conflict situations. MAGTFs are balanced, combined arms forces with organic command, ground, aviation, and sustainment ele- ments.

MAGTFs are organized, trained, and equipped to perform forward-presence, crisis-response, and full-scale combat missions, including forcible entry by amphibious assault. With the exception of special purpose MAGTFs (discussed later), MAGTFs are general-purpose air-ground-logistics forces that can be tailored to the requirements of a specific situation.

Marines routinely organize, train, deploy, and operate as MAGTFs. The MAGTF is a modular organization tailorable to each mission. Most military organizations are specifically designed for particular missions, and reorganization tends to reduce their effectiveness. However, the Marine Corps' building-block approach to MAGTF organization makes reorganization a matter of routine. Tailoring MAGTFs for specific missions through task organization is standard procedure. As a result, the MAGTF is a cohesive military organization with well-understood command relationships and operating procedures.

MAGTFs can perform missions ranging from humanitarian assistance to peacekeeping to intense combat and can operate in permissive, uncertain, and hostile environments. MAGTFs can operate from sea or expeditionary bases, or both. Depending on the requirements of the situation, they can present minimal presence ashore or a highly visible presence. They can project combat power ashore in measured degrees as needed and can provide secure staging areas ashore for follow-on forces. In this way, sea-based MAGTFs provide the National Command Authorities and combatant commanders a "rheostat" of options and capabilities to vary the composition, scope, and size of the forces phased ashore.

THE STRUCTURE OF THE MAGTF

While MAGTFs are task-organized, each MAGTF, regardless of size or mission, has the same basic structure. Each MAGTF has four core elements: a command element, ground combat element, aviation combat element, and combat service support element. The MAGTF's combat forces reside within these four elements. (See figure page 71.)

The command element provides the command and control necessary for the effective planning and execution of all military operations. It is normally a permanent headquarters. It

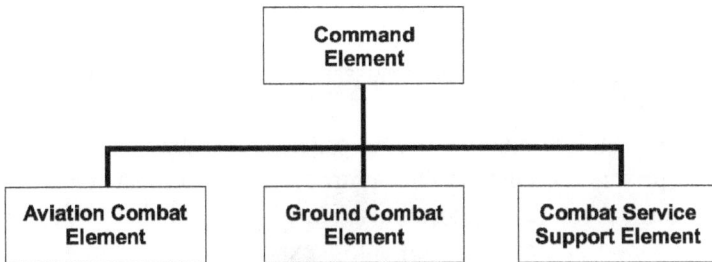

Structure of the MAGTF.

also includes units that provide intelligence, communications, and administrative support in general support of the MAGTF.

The ground combat element is task-organized to conduct ground operations in support of the MAGTF mission. During amphibious operations, it projects ground combat power ashore using transport helicopters from the aviation combat element and organic and Navy landing craft. It may have any composition required by the mission, although normally it is built around an infantry unit reinforced with artillery, reconnaissance, armor, engineer, and other forces as needed. The ground combat element may range from a light, air-transportable unit to one that is relatively heavy and mechanized.

The aviation combat element is task-organized to support the MAGTF mission by performing some or all of the six functions of Marine aviation: antiair warfare, assault support, offensive air support, air reconnaissance, electronic warfare, and control of aircraft and missiles. The aviation combat element is normally built around an aircraft organization augmented with appropriate air command and control, combat, combat support, and combat service support units. The aviation combat element can operate effectively from ships, expeditionary airfields, or austere forward operating sites and can readily and routinely transit between sea bases and expeditionary airfields without loss of capability. The aviation combat element can range in size and composition from an aviation detachment with specific capabilities to one or more Marine aircraft wings.

The combat service support element is task-organized to provide a full range of support functions from sea bases aboard naval shipping or from expeditionary bases ashore. The combat service support element provides sustainment for the MAGTF. It can also provide logistical support external to the MAGTF, as in disaster relief operations, for example. MAGTFs can augment this organic sustainability by external support from Navy, other-Service, and host nation support organizations.

One of the key features of Marine expeditionary organization is expandability. Because of the frequent need for rapid response, the initial force at the scene of a developing crisis may not be the decisive force. Crisis response requires the ability to expand the expeditionary force after its introduction in theater without sacrificing the continuity of operational capability. The MAGTF's modular structure lends itself to rapidly and easily expanding into a larger force as a situation demands by simply adding forces as needed to the core units of each existing element. This expandability includes expanding into a joint or combined force, because the generic MAGTF structure parallels the structure of a multidimensional joint force.

THE MARINE EXPEDITIONARY FORCE

The Marine expeditionary force (MEF) is the principal Marine Corps warfighting organization, particularly for larger crises or contingencies. It is capable of missions across the range of military operations, including amphibious assault and sustained operations ashore in any environment.

The three standing Marine expeditionary forces—I, II, and III MEFs—are each located near airports, railheads, and ports for rapid deployment. Each Marine expeditionary force consists of a permanent command element and one Marine division, Marine aircraft wing, and force service support group. Each forward-deploys Marine expeditionary units on a continual basis.

The size and composition of a deployed Marine expeditionary force can vary greatly depending on the requirements of the mission. A Marine expeditionary force can deploy with not only its own units but also units from the other standing Marine expeditionary forces, the Marine Corps Reserve, or other Services. For example, I Marine Expeditionary Force in Operation Desert Storm included 1st and 2d Marine Divisions, 1st and 2d Force Service Support Groups, 3d Marine Aircraft Wing reinforced with groups and squadrons from the 1st and 2d Marine Aircraft Wings, elements from Marine Forces Reserve, and the U.S. Army's "Tiger" Brigade. A Marine expeditionary force typically deploys with 60 days of sustainment.

A Marine expeditionary force normally deploys by echelon. The lead echelon of the Marine expeditionary force, tailored to meet a specific mission, is designated the Marine expeditionary force (Forward) and may be commanded by the Marine expeditionary force commander personally or by a designated commander. The Marine expeditionary force (forward) prepares for the subsequent arrival of the rest of the Marine expeditionary force or other joint or combined forces. However, the deployment of the Marine expeditionary force (forward) does not necessarily mean that all the forces of the standing Marine expeditionary force will follow. This would occur only if the entire Marine expeditionary force were required.

THE MARINE EXPEDITIONARY UNIT (SPECIAL OPERATIONS CAPABLE)

The Marine expeditionary unit (special operations capable (MEU(SOC)) is the standard forward-deployed Marine expeditionary organization. Though each Marine expeditionary unit (special operations capable) is task-organized, a typical Marine expeditionary unit includes—

- A standing command element.

- An infantry battalion reinforced with artillery, reconnaissance, engineer, armor, and assault amphibian units.

- A reinforced helicopter squadron with transport, utility, and attack helicopters, a detachment of vertical/short takeoff and landing (V/STOL) fixed-wing attack aircraft, and other detachments as required.

- A task-organized combat service support element.

- Sustainment for 15 days.

Marine expeditionary units (special operations capable) undergo intensive predeployment training and are augmented with selected personnel and equipment to provide enhanced capabilities such as specialized demolition operations, clandestine reconnaissance and surveillance, raids, and in-extremis hostage recovery.

Marine Corps Forces Atlantic and Pacific maintain forward-deployed Marine expeditionary units (special operations capable) in the Mediterranean Sea, the western Pacific, and the Indian Ocean or Persian Gulf region. The Marine expeditionary unit (special operations capable) can be thought of both as a self-contained operating force capable of missions of limited scope and duration and as a forward-deployed extension of the Marine expeditionary force. Deployed with an amphibious ready group, the Marine expeditionary unit (special operations capable) provides either a combatant commander in chief or other operational commander a quick, sea-based reaction force for a wide variety of situations. In many cases, the Marine expeditionary unit (special operations capable) embarked on amphibious shipping will be the first U.S. force at the scene of a crisis and can conduct enabling actions for larger follow-on forces, whether a Marine expeditionary force, joint task force, or some other force. It can provide a visible and credible presence in many potential trouble spots and can demonstrate the United States' willingness to protect its interests overseas. The Marine expeditionary unit (special operations capable) has a limited forcible entry capability.

THE SPECIAL PURPOSE MAGTF

A special purpose MAGTF (SPMAGTF) may be formed to conduct a specific mission that is limited in scope and focus and often in duration. A special purpose MAGTF may be any size, but normally it is a relatively small force—the size of a Marine expeditionary unit or smaller—with narrowly focused capabilities chosen to accomplish a limited mission. Common missions of a special purpose MAGTF include raids, peacekeeping, noncombatant evacuation, disaster relief, and humanitarian assistance. For example, a special purpose MAGTF was deployed to Haiti to restore democracy, conduct peacekeeping operations, and provide humanitarian assistance. Special purpose MAGTFs are normally designated by the mission location or operation name, such as "SPMAGTF Somalia" or "SPMAGTF Support Democracy."

A special purpose MAGTF may be task-organized deliberately from the assets of a standing Marine expeditionary force and deployed from its home base for a particular mission, or it may be formed on a contingency basis from an already-deployed MAGTF to perform an independent, rapid-response mission of usually limited scope and duration. An example of the former is SPMAGTF Liberia, which was formed from elements of the II Marine Expeditionary Force and deployed from Camp Lejeune, North Carolina, to relieve the 22d Marine Expeditionary Unit (special operations capable) deployed off the coast of Liberia in April 1996. An example of the latter is the special purpose MAGTF that conducted Operation Eastern Exit, the evacuation of the U.S. Embassy in Mogadishu, Somalia, in January 1991.[7] It was formed from elements of the 4th Marine Expeditionary Brigade, deployed in the Gulf of Oman for Operations Desert Shield and Desert Storm in 1990–1991.

MARITIME PREPOSITIONING FORCES

Maritime prepositioning forces are a key element of the Marine Corps' expeditionary capability. The deployment of expeditionary forces rapidly to practically any part of the globe is made possible through the linkup of personnel from the operating forces with prepositioned equipment and supplies. A maritime prepositioning force consists of two basic building blocks:

- Prepositioned shipping carrying equipment and supplies.

- Marines and Sailors, with selected items of equipment, flown into the objective area by strategic airlift to link up with the equipment. Depending on the mission, the fly-in echelon can include some 120 self-deploying air- craft.

There are three maritime prepositioning ships squadrons. Each squadron consists of four or five multipurpose vessels. These squadrons are maintained at strategic locations around the globe that allow at least one of them to steam to any part of the world within a matter of days. The equipment on a single maritime prepositioning ships squadron is the equivalent of more than 3,000 airlift sorties.

Each maritime prepositioning ships squadron contains equipment and 30 days of sustainment for nearly 18,000 Marines from one of the standing Marine expeditionary forces task-organized around a Marine infantry regiment, a Marine aircraft group, and a combat service support element. These forces, along with a Navy support element, fly into the theater using 250 strategic airlift sorties and link up with the equipment unloaded from the prepositioning ships. Within a few days, any combatant commander can have the lead echelon of a Marine expeditionary force ready for employment.

Maritime prepositioning forces can deploy in conjunction with a forward-deployed amphibious force that secures the linkup site, or it can deploy independently where a secure arrival and assembly area already exists. With the capability to offload pierside or at sea, the maritime prepositioning force MAGTF can go ashore with minimal or nonexistent port facilities.

Maritime prepositioning forces can provide a variety of employment options to a combatant commander. Through designated offload from prepositioning ships in concert with a tailored fly-in echelon, a commander can task-organize to—

- Deploy a MAGTF weighted to provide a specific capability, such as support to a military operation other than war.

- Augment the capabilities of an on-the-scene Marine expeditionary unit (special operations capable) by providing additional equipment.

- Selectively reinforce a Marine expeditionary unit (special operations capable) or air contingency MAGTF by providing mixes of Marines and equipment that can be absorbed into the unit's command, ground combat, aviation combat, and combat service support elements.

By combining all three maritime prepositioning ships squadrons, the entire combat power of a heavy, mechanized Marine expeditionary force can be deployed to a region.

The ultimate usefulness of maritime prepositioning forces is their enormous flexibility. Through a building-block approach, they provide combatant commanders a cost-effec- tive, rapid, sustainable global crisis response capability that can be employed across a wide range of expeditionary opera- tions.

AIR CONTINGENCY FORCES

Air contingency forces may be dispatched to respond to fast-developing crises. An air contingency MAGTF is an on-call, combat-ready task organization that can begin deployment by strategic airlift within 18 hours of notification. The fixed wing aircraft of the air contingency MAGTF will normally self-deploy. Both Marine Corps Forces Atlantic and Marine Corps Forces Pacific maintain air contingency MAGTFs in a continuous state of readiness. These forces require a secure airfield at the point of entry. The air contingency MAGTF that deploys will be task-organized based on the mission, threat, and available airlift. Its size can range from a reinforced rifle company with a small combat service support element to a MAGTF with a regimental-size ground combat element and appropriate aviation and combat service support elements.

An air contingency MAGTF can deploy independently or in conjunction with a Marine expeditionary unit (special operations capable), maritime prepositioning force, or other expeditionary force. Unlike maritime prepositioning force troops who deploy without most of their organic equipment in anticipation of marrying up in theater with that from the maritime prepositioning squadrons, air contingency forces must deploy to the theater with all of the organic equipment they require. Also unlike maritime prepositioning forces, air contingency forces do not have an organic sustainment capability.

MARINE CORPS COMPONENT COMMANDS

All joint forces include Service components. A component is one of the subordinate organizations that constitute a joint force. A Service component command consists of the Service component commander and all those individuals, units, detachments, organizations, and installations under that command that are assigned to a joint force—that is, to a combatant command, subordinate unified command, or joint task force.[8]

The Service component commander is responsible in the operational chain of command to the joint force commander and in the administrative chain of command to the respective Service chief. The Marine Corps component commander deals directly with the joint force commander in matters affecting assigned Marine forces. The Marine Corps component commander commands, trains, equips, and sustains all Marine component forces. In general, the Marine Corps component commander is responsible for—

- Advising the joint force commander on the use of Marine Corps forces.

- Accomplishing missions or tasks assigned by the joint force commander.

- Informing the joint force commander as to the situation and progress of assigned Marine Corps forces.

- Providing Service-specific support—administrative, logistical, training, and intelligence—to assigned Marine Corps forces.

There are two levels of Marine Corps components: a Marine Corps component commander under command of a combatant commander or a subunified commander, and a Marine Corps component commander under command of a joint task force commander. A Marine Corps component commander under a combatant commander may have one or more MAGTFs assigned, as well as other required theater-level organizations. For example, a Marine Logistic Command might be established to provide theater logistical support for all Marine forces, freeing the combat service support element of each MAGTF to focus internally on MAGTF combat service support requirements.

When so designated by the joint force commander, a Marine Corps component commander may also serve as a functional component commander. A functional component command is a command that is normally composed of forces of two or more Military Departments. It may be established to perform particular operational missions.[9] Joint force commanders may establish functional component commanders (i.e., joint force air component commander, joint force land component commander, joint force maritime component commander, and joint force special operations component commander) to conduct operations or employ them primarily to coordinate selected functions. Normally, the component commander with the preponderance of forces or the requisite command and control capability to perform the required mis- sion is designated the functional component commander. A Marine Corps component commander designated as a functional component commander retains Service component command responsibilities. Due to the unique nature of Marine Corps forces assigned to a joint force, the Marine Corps component commander may be designated as the joint force maritime, land, or air component commander.

MAGTFs operate effectively under the operational control of either the Marine Corps component commander or a functional component commander. However, exercise of operational control through the Marine Corps component commander normally takes greater advantage of established chains of command, maintains the operational integrity of Marine Corps forces, exploits common Service doctrine and operating methods, and facilitates the coordination of operating and support requirements.

CONCLUSION

The Marine Corps provides a variety of versatile, deployable, and expandable organizations specifically designed to conduct or support expeditionary operations. The MAGTF, a modular task organization of air, ground, and logistics elements, is the Marine Corps' basic operating organization. MAGTFs can deploy rapidly as part of amphibious ready forces, maritime prepositioning forces, or air contingency forces. Coming in a variety of sizes and capabilities, they provide a combatant commander or other operational commander with a responsive and adaptive expeditionary capability suitable for satisfying a broad range of operational needs.

Chapter 4

Expeditionary Concepts

"A Military, Naval, Littoral War, when wisely prepared and discreetly conducted, is a terrible Sort of War. Happy for that People who are Sovereigns enough of the Sea to put it into Execution! For it comes like Thunder and lightning to some unprepared Part of the World."[1]

—Thomas More Molyneux, 1759

"Ever since the days of the Phoenicians, the ability to land on defended shores has been a source of strength for those who possess it and a source of concern for those who must oppose it."[2]

—Robert H. Barrow

This chapter describes the Marine Corps' fundamental operating concepts for the conduct of expeditionary operations: operational maneuver from the sea, sustained operations ashore, military operations other than war, and maritime prepositioning force operations. The applicable concept in any given instance depends on the particular political and military conditions. All of these expeditionary concepts are compatible with the fundamental Marine Corps doctrine of maneuver warfare.

OPERATIONAL MANEUVER FROM THE SEA

The capstone operating concept for Marine Corps expeditionary operations is *Operational Maneuver from the Sea.*[3] This concept describes the maneuver of naval forces at the operational level in a maritime implementation of Marine Corps maneuver warfare doctrine across the range of military operations—from major theater war to military operations other than war.

Operational maneuver from the sea is an amphibious operation that seeks to use the sea as an avenue for maneuvering against some operational-level objective.[4] The concept recognizes the requirement for forcible entry—an amphibious landing in the face of organized military resistance—although not all operational maneuvers from the sea entail forcible entry.

The concept envisions the MAGTF operating as part of a naval expeditionary force conducting operations as part of a theater or joint task force campaign. Operational maneuver from the sea may or may not develop into sustained operations ashore.

Operational maneuver from the sea is not limited to combat at the high end of the range of military operations. In fact, one of the principles of operational maneuver from the sea is to use the mobility provided by naval power to avoid enemy strengths and strike where the enemy is weak. Many operational maneuvers from the sea will be conducted during military operations other than war.

By definition, an operational maneuver from the sea involves the entry phase of an expeditionary operation. It may also include enabling actions or decisive actions, depending on the nature of the situation. In other words, the operational maneuver may be intended to set the stage for the decisive action, or it may itself constitute the decisive move.

As the title of the concept denotes, there are two main aspects to operational maneuver from the sea. The first is operational maneuver, the employment of the MAGTF as an operational-level force in such a way as to gain and exploit an operational advantage. Classically, this has often meant using the sea as a means for turning the enemy's flank and threatening his lines of operations. For example, in one brilliant stroke, General MacArthur's landing of the 1st Marine Division at Inchon to attack Seoul in 1950 turned the tide of the Korean

War. It cut off the North Korean army's lines of communications at Seoul and facilitated 8th Army's breakout from the Pusan perimeter. The Allied landing at Salerno, Italy, in 1944, although predictable and not well executed, sought to bypass Axis defenses in southern Italy rather than attack frontally the length of the peninsula. Another example of operational maneuver was Operation Galvanic, the bloody assault of Tarawa in November 1943, which secured a jumping-off point for the campaign to seize the operationally important Marshall Islands. Possession of the Marshalls in turn facilitated the decisive penetration of the heart of the Japanese defenses in the Marianas.

Operational maneuver from the sea is not merely a way of introducing an expeditionary force onto foreign soil, although it does that, but a way of projecting expeditionary power directly against some center of gravity or critical vulnerability. The idea is to use the operational mobility of naval power to launch an attack at the time and place of our choosing to exploit an enemy weakness.

Operational maneuver from the sea includes the implementing concept of ship-to-objective maneuver. Historically, amphibious operations have involved creating an initial lodgment on a foreign shore, followed by a buildup of combat power and supplies on an established beachhead. The ship-to-shore movement was primarily a way of transferring combat power ashore. The choice of landing beach was necessarily dictated largely by the technical and tactical problems of getting ashore safely. Only after sufficient combat power and supplies had been placed ashore could the landing force launch its attack against its main objective ashore, which was its reason for landing in the first place. This buildup of combat power also gave the enemy time to strengthen his defenses, nullifying any advantages in tempo and surprise the attacker had gained. Frequently, this warning and consequent reinforcement compelled the landing force to plan and fight a deliberate and often costly pitched battle to break out of the beachhead. Made possible primarily by advances in the technology for transporting landing forces ashore, the operational maneuver from the sea concept seeks to generate operating tempo by combining the ship-to-shore movement and what has traditionally been called "subsequent operations ashore" into a single, decisive maneuver directly from the ship.

It may not always be possible to maneuver directly against operational objectives. However, even where objectives are tactical, we should seek to exploit the mobility and firepower provided by naval power and the ability to introduce ground combat power quickly to attack rapidly at a time and place of our own choosing before the enemy can respond adequately. As an example, on the morning of 25 October 1983, the 22d Marine Amphibious Unit launched a helicopterborne assault to capture Pearls and Grenville on the northeast coast of Grenada in Operation Urgent Fury. The same unit exploited the operational mobility provided by Amphibious Squadron 4 to launch an unplanned surfaceborne assault at Grand Mal Bay on the west side of the island later the same day.

The second main aspect of operational maneuver from the sea is "from the sea." The operational maneuver from the sea concept seeks to fully exploit the naval character of Marine Corps forces—their ability to move by sea, deploy at sea near the scene of a crisis, project power ashore and sustain themselves from the sea, and redeploy to the sea. What distinguishes operational maneuver from the sea is the use of the sea as a means of gaining operational advantage, as an avenue for friendly movement that is simultaneously a barrier to the enemy, and as a means of avoiding disadvantageous engagements.

Sea basing is an important implementing concept of operational maneuver from the sea. Sea basing applies to fire support, command and control, and other functions as well as to logistics. However, sea basing is not an absolute requirement for operational maneuver from the sea; support may also be based ashore as each situation dictates.

The operational maneuver from the sea concept envisions that most or all aviation—especially fixed-wing aviation— will remain sea based during the evolution. Likewise, some or most logistics will remain sea based. Sea-based logistics does not mean that ground units will not carry unit-level supplies; it means that most landing-force-level logistics, including supply dumps and repair facilities, will remain afloat. The operational maneuver from the sea concept also envisions that most MAGTF command and control will remain afloat rather than ashore. However, some command and control in support of the ground combat element will be passed ashore as the situation requires. Finally, the concept envisions that the landing force will be supported by naval surface fires to augment its own land-based fire support.

Sea basing done properly can be a source of operational freedom of action. Historically, the tactical and operational options available to landing forces were constrained by the need to establish, employ, and protect large supply dumps ashore. These logistical bases dictated and limited operational direction and range. With the increased use of sea basing, the logistics tail of landing forces will be smaller, subsequent operations ashore can start without the traditional buildup phase within the beachhead, and landing forces will have greater operational freedom of action. The important results can be an increase in operating tempo and reduced requirements for rear area security. The reduction of the support infrastructure ashore will also facilitate the rapid redeployment of the landing force. All of this helps the landing force avoid combat on unfavorable terms.

CASE STUDY: THE MARIANAS, 1944

Operation Forager, the U.S. invasion of the Marianas Islands in the summer of 1944 during the Second World War, provides a classic example of operational maneuver from the sea.[5] The Allied strategy in the Pacific called for a two-prong counteroffensive: General MacArthur would advance generally northwest out of Australia in the southwest Pacific theater of operations while Admiral Nimitz drove west out of Hawaii in the central Pacific. While MacArthur was starting his New Guinea drive in early 1944, Nimitz moved on the heavily fortified Marshalls in the central Pacific. The key island of Kwajalein fell on 7 February, and Eniwetok, the westernmost garrison, was captured by 21 February. The Joint Chiefs approved Nimitz's recommendation to bypass Truk in the Carolines and instead to attack the Marianas in June. The stage was now set for Operation Forager.

The Marianas were of significant strategic importance. Considered part of the Japanese homeland, their capture by the Allies would have an important political and psychological effect on both sides. Moreover, this maneuver into the heart of the Japanese defenses threatened Japanese north-south lines of communications. Allied possession of the Marianas isolated the Carolines to the south and endangered Japanese sea lines of communication to Rabaul in New Guinea and Truk. Control of the Carolines was essential to protecting the right flank of MacArthur's upcoming invasion of the Philippines. It was also of significant military importance that possession of the Marianas exposed most of the remaining Japanese positions and opened more operational options to the Allies than the Japanese could defend against: south to the Carolines and Truk, southwest to the Palaus, west to the Philippines, northwest to Okinawa, or north to the Volcanoes and Bonins. Finally, the Marianas provided air bases for long-range air strikes against the Japanese mainland. (See figure.)

Nimitz assigned operational command of Forager to Admiral Raymond Spruance, commander of the U.S. 5th Fleet. Spruance organized three main forces:

- The Joint Expeditionary Force including, as its Expeditionary Troops, General Holland M. Smith's V Amphibious Corps of 127,000 troops.

- Task Force 58, the Fast-Carrier Attack Force, under Admiral Marc Mitscher.

- All U.S. Army, Navy, and Marine land-based aircraft assigned to support the operation, including the Army's 7th Air Force, under Navy command.

The military objectives were three of the southernmost Marianas islands, Saipan, Tinian, and Guam. The northernmost, Saipan, would be attacked first to deny airfields to any Japanese air support flying from Iwo Jima in the Volcanoes or from mainland Japan. Saipan was more than a thousand miles from Eniwetok in the Marshalls, the nearest U.S. advanced naval base. This would be by far the longest amphibious projection attempted yet in the war. Previously, amphibious advances had been limited to about 300 miles, the range of land-based fighters providing close air support. In Operation Forager, all

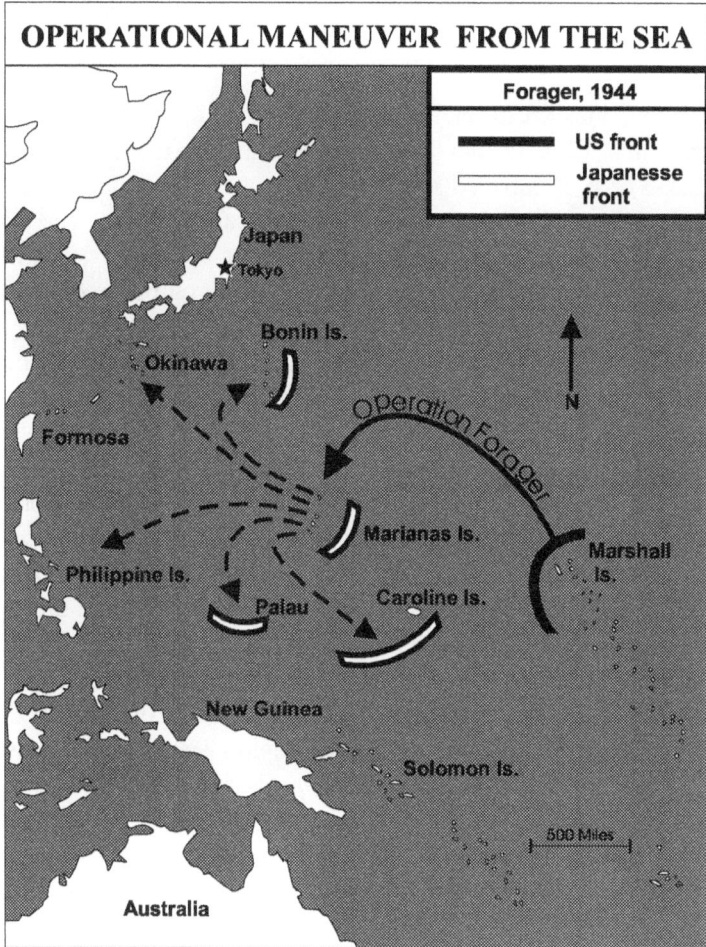

OPERATIONAL MANEUVER FROM THE SEA

Forager, 1944

US front

Japanesse front

Japan
★ Tokyo

Bonin Is.

Okinawa

Formosa

N

Operation Forager

Marianas Is.

Philippine Is.

Palau

Caroline Is.

Marshall Is.

New Guinea

Solomon Is.

500 Miles

Australia

close air support would be sea-based, flying off Task Force 58's carriers.

The Joint Expeditionary Force assembled in California, Hawaii, and Guadalcanal and rendezvoused in the Marshalls. Task Force 58 arrived east of Guam on 11 June and commenced bombardment with aviation and naval gunfire. The 2d and 4th Marine Divisions landed abreast at Saipan on 15 June against heavy resistance. They made slow progress, requiring the Guam landing to be delayed by a month. Saipan was finally secured on 13 July; the Guam landing began on 21 July and the Tinian landing on 24 July. After tough fighting, Guam was declared secured on 10 August.

There was only limited latitude for tactical maneuver ashore, although both Saipan and Tinian involved the use of amphibious feints, and the Tinian operation achieved tactical surprise. Nevertheless, all three landings amounted to hard-fought direct assaults against fortified defenses. The real significance of the Forager landings was their direct operational and strategic effect. The Marianas operation pierced the inner defenses that Japan had constructed to defend its empire. The cabinet led by General Tojo was forced to resign in disgrace. By November, B-29 bombers operating from Saipan were attacking Japan on a daily basis, eventually reaching a rate of over a thousand sorties a week. Although the war in the Pacific continued for another year after Forager, this operational maneuver from the sea against the Marianas had sealed Japan's ultimate fate.

This case study illustrates that operational maneuver from the sea is not a new concept dependent on emerging technology but instead has a strong historical basis. Some of the most effective employments of amphibious forces and operations throughout history have been to conduct operational and even strategic maneuver. That said, due to recent advances in doctrine, techniques, and technology, current operating capabilities greatly exceed those of 1944. As these advances continue, capabilities will continue to improve. The fictional case study starting on page 125 illustrates the potential future application of operational maneuver from the sea and other expeditionary concepts.

SUSTAINED OPERATIONS ASHORE

While organized and equipped to participate in naval campaigns, the Marine Corps has frequently been called on to conduct sustained operations ashore. From the American Civil War to the Vietnam War to the Gulf War, Marine Corps forces have participated in operations in which their naval character and their relations with the Navy played a limited role.

Today's sustained operations ashore are those extended operations, usually of significant scale, in which MAGTFs fight not as amphibious or sea-based naval forces, but essentially as land forces. This concept envisions that Marine Corps forces are part of a larger joint or combined force with the Marine Corps forces operating under the Marine Corps Service component or a functional land component.

During sustained operations ashore, Marine Corps forces will use the sea to complement their land-based operational mobility—including shore-to-shore or even ship-to-shore operations. MAGTFs conducting sustained operations ashore may employ a combination of sea- or land-based fires, logistics, and command and control support—depending upon the situation.

In sustained operations ashore, MAGTFs are often best employed as independent formations that are assigned operational or tactical missions appropriate to a self-contained, self-sustaining combined arms force with both air and ground capabilities. Operational maneuver is as integral to sustained operations ashore as it is to operational maneuver from the sea. Appropriate missions include advance force, covering force, and enabling force operations, independent supporting attacks, and employment as an operational reserve or operational maneuver element. Depending on the nature and scale of operations, a MAGTF may constitute or compose part of an enabling force or a decisive force. A MAGTF engaged in sustained operations ashore may include elements from other Services or countries, as I Marine Expeditionary Force included the British 7 Armour Brigade during Operation Desert

Shield and the U.S. Army "Tiger" Brigade during Operation Desert Storm.

Sustained operations ashore may follow an operational maneuver from the sea when the amphibious operation is a way of introducing forces into a theater for a sustained campaign. The Allied landings in Normandy in 1944, for example, were the opening move in Eisenhower's campaign in Europe, in contrast to the Forager landings, started 9 days later in the Marianas, which were part of a series of landings conducted during Nimitz's campaign in the central Pacific.

Currently when sustained operations ashore follow an amphibious operation, a transition must generally be made from sea basing to land basing. This transition is a complex undertaking involving the phasing ashore of various command and support functions. Future technology and mobility enhancements will allow the Marine Corps to execute ship-to-objective maneuver. Ship-to-objective maneuver reduces the footprint ashore, provides greater security to the force, and allows the force to sea base many of the command and support functions previously transitioned ashore.

CASE STUDY: THE PERSIAN GULF, 1990–1991

Iraq invaded Kuwait on 2 August 1990.[6] On 7 August, President Bush ordered 125,000 troops to the Persian Gulf as part of a multinational force with the initial mission of protecting Saudi Arabia. Designated Desert Shield, the U.S. operation was under the command of the Commander in Chief, U.S. Central Command, General H. Norman Schwarzkopf. Among the U.S. forces was I Marine Expeditionary Force based in Camp Pendleton, California, which arrived at the beginning of September under the command of Lieutenant General Walter E. Boomer. Lieutenant General Boomer was also designated as Central Command's Marine Corps component commander, responsible directly to General Schwarzkopf for the operations of all Marine Corps forces save those assigned to the Navy component as landing forces. The Marine Corps component was assigned the mission of defending the Jubayl sector throughout the duration of Desert Shield. (See figure.)

The 3d Marine Aircraft Wing established its headquarters at Shaikh Isa Air Base as I Marine Expeditionary Force's aviation combat element. Marine aviation during Desert Shield/Desert Storm was based ashore, except for the aviation belonging to MAGTFs assigned to the Navy component. Aircraft squadrons were based ashore at several military and civilian airfields.

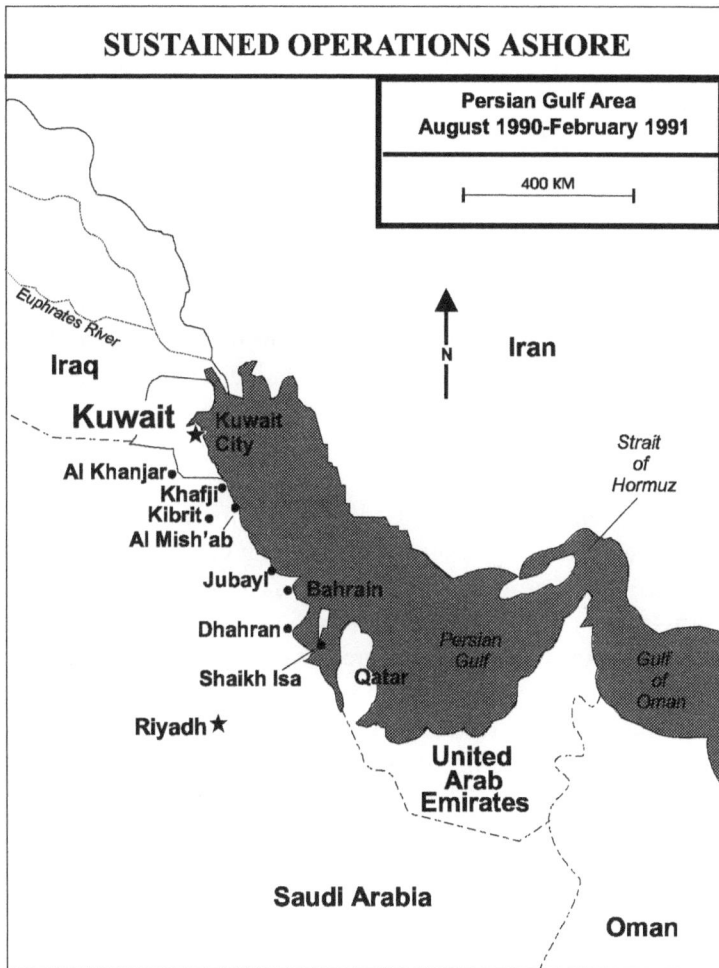

One of the first and most difficult issues to be worked out was the control of Marine aviation. An agreement was reached with the commander of U.S. Air Forces Central Command. The joint force air component commander would issue a daily air tasking order to coordinate all theater air operations. Marine aviation would support the Marine Corps forces while providing a percentage of its fixed-wing sorties to Central Command for theater missions. In turn, joint force air component commander sorties would strike deep targets nominated by the Marine Corps component. To ensure the responsive close air support traditionally enjoyed by Marine ground forces, the Marine Corps component would control offensive air missions within its area of operations.

By the end of October, planning began for an offensive operation to liberate Kuwait. Initial planning called for I Marine Expeditionary Force to be treated as if it were an Army corps—employed to create a breach in the Iraqi barrier through which the Army mechanized forces would pass—with most of its organic aviation employed in support of non-Marine units. Lieutenant General Boomer argued for more effective employment of the Marine expeditionary force, and General Schwarzkopf agreed. The Marines would launch a supporting attack toward Kuwait City.

Eventually, I Marine Expeditionary Force was given the mission "to conduct a supporting attack to penetrate Iraqi defenses, destroy Iraqi forces in its zone of action, and secure key objectives to prevent reinforcement of Iraqi forces facing the

Joint Forces Command-North/Northern Area Command. Once this was achieved, I Marine Expeditionary Force was to establish blocking positions to halt the northerly retreat of Iraqi forces from southeastern Kuwait and Kuwait City and to assist passage of Coalition Forces in Kuwait City."[7] On the Marine expeditionary force's right flank would be Joint Forces Command East, comprising five Arab mechanized brigades. On the Marine expeditionary force's left flank would be Joint Forces Command North, another Arab force. Farther west as part of Central Command's main attack was the heavily armored U.S. VII Corps, which had arrived from Germany in November. Farther west still, also part of the flanking attack, was the U.S. XVIII Corps. (See figure, page 106.)[8]

An offensive operation would require more forces, and reinforcements to I Marine Expeditionary Force started arriving in December. The 2d Marine Division arrived from North Carolina to constitute a second maneuver element in the ground combat element. Elements of 2d Marine Aircraft Wing arrived from North Carolina to reinforce 3d Marine Aircraft Wing, now increased to 32 aircraft squadrons.

With the arrival of 2d Force Service Support Group, Lieutenant General Boomer reorganized his logistics. The 1st Force Service Support Group assumed the role of general support logistics for all Marine Corps forces from the port at Jubayl to the combat service support area. The newly arrived 2d Force Service Support Group became the Direct Support Command, responsible for direct support of the divisions and forward

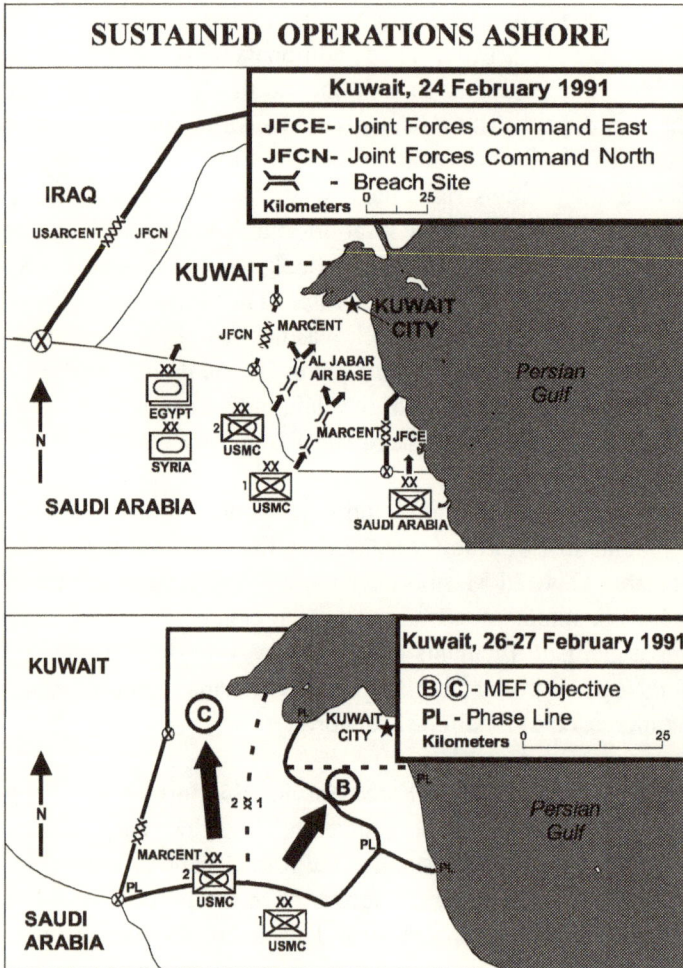

SUSTAINED OPERATIONS ASHORE

Kuwait, 24 February 1991

JFCE- Joint Forces Command East
JFCN- Joint Forces Command North
— - Breach Site
Kilometers 0   25

Kuwait, 26-27 February 1991

B C- MEF Objective
PL - Phase Line
Kilometers 0   25

aviation units from the combat service support area to the front.

Headquarters Marine Corps also activated 80 units of the Selected Marine Corps Reserve, more than half the personnel of the 4th Division-Wing team. The largest Reserve unit mobilized was the 24th Marines, which in January 1991 assumed responsibility for rear area security.

Offensive air operations commenced on 17 January for the purpose of knocking out Iraq's command and control and transportation systems and attacking the Republican Guards. The ground offensive began on 24 February. First Marine Expeditionary Force's two divisions attacked abreast, 2d on the left and 1st on the right. The plan was to penetrate into the depth of the Iraqi defensive system at an identified weak point at the "elbow" of Kuwait in order to outflank the prepared defensive positions and quickly destroy Iraqi operational reserves. The 1st Division attacked toward Al Jaber Airfield. It would continue the attack to capture Marine expeditionary force Objective B, Kuwait International Airport, in order to isolate Kuwait City. The 2d Division would attack toward Marine expeditionary force Objective C, the main supply route intersections near Al Jahrah, some 33 kilometers west of Kuwait City, in order to prevent Iraqi forces from escaping west and north. (See figure.)[9]

By 26 February, I Marine Expeditionary Force's units were closing in on their objectives. That morning, aircraft from

Marine Aircraft Group 11 and Marine Aircraft Group 13 attacked more than a thousand Iraqi vehicles trying to escape north on the highway from Al Jahrah. Marine Aircraft Group 11 alone flew 298 sorties. By that afternoon, 2d Marine Division had captured Al Jahrah. Early on 27 February, elements of 1st Division secured Kuwait International Airport and then halted while the Arab Joint Forces Command entered Kuwait City.

By now, Central Command's flanking attack had reached the Euphrates River. Iraqi resistance was disintegrating. On 28 February, President Bush declared a cease-fire. The ground offensive had lasted 100 hours.

In both the defensive operations of Desert Shield and the offensive operations of Desert Storm, in both ground and air operations, Marine Corps forces designed for naval operations proved their worth in sustained operations ashore fighting side-by-side with mechanized and armored forces designed specifically for mobile, desert warfare.

MILITARY OPERATIONS OTHER THAN WAR

The concept of military operations other than war encompasses the use of military capabilities across the range of military operations short of war. These military actions can be applied to complement any combination of the other instruments of national power and occur before, during, and after war.[10]

Not all military operations other than war take place in a permissive environment or even a relatively safe one. The situation may be almost completely permissive, as in, for example, disaster relief situations in which the disaster has not led to social or political disorder. However, military operations other than war may also take place in environments characterized by widespread random violence or even combat of less than large scale.

In military operations other than war more than in war, political concerns tend to restrict the application of military force. Political considerations may even necessitate military actions or deployments that are not militarily advantageous. Rules of engagement will often greatly restrict military action. In many cases, it is difficult to identify clear and finite military objectives that constitute the measure of success.

Military operations other than war generally require closer coordination with the host nation government, other nonmilitary agencies, and the local populace than do conventional, large-scale combat operations. Furthermore, the types of situations that lead to military operations other than war are generally of significant interest to the media and generally allow greater access than do combat situations. As a result, many military operations other than war require military forces to deal with the media daily or more frequently than in conventional combat operations.

The types of missions that constitute military operations other than war have historically been Marine Corps missions. They are generally directed at limited objectives and are often of limited duration. As conducted by the Marine Corps, most military operations other than war apply the principles of operational maneuver from the sea. That is, they involve the use of the sea for strategic, operational, and even tactical mobility to project military force against some center of gravity or critical vulnerability at the time and place of our choosing. Most involve sea basing or at least some sea-based support.

Common examples of military operations other than war include—

- Noncombatant evacuation operations.
- Humanitarian assistance, to relieve the effects of natural or manmade disasters.
- Peacekeeping, to monitor and implement an existing truce.
- Peacemaking, or military intervention to establish peace between belligerents who may or may not be engaged in actual combat.

- Counterterrorism, counterdrug, and security operations, either in the form of technical support to law enforcement agencies or as purely military actions.

- Mobile training teams, to provide in-country military instruction to host nation personnel.

MAGTFs conduct military operations other than war as part of a joint or combined task force. The MAGTF may serve as the nucleus for such a task force. However, given the extremely wide range of military operations other than war, there will be a correspondingly wide range of command relationships. For example, a Marine Corps mobile training team may be assigned to a military advisory group, or a Fleet antiterrorism security team may be assigned to reinforce a Marine security guard detachment.

CASE STUDY: MOGADISHU, SOMALIA, 1991

The evacuation of the U.S. Embassy in Mogadishu, Somalia, in January 1991 is just one example of military operations other than war that Marine expeditionary forces can routinely be expected to conduct.[11] Somalia's long-simmering civil war had worsened throughout the fall of 1990. On 2 January 1991, U.S. Ambassador James K. Bishop requested military assistance for evacuation of the embassy.

The mission fell to U.S. Central Command, which already had numerous forces deployed to the Persian Gulf for Operations Desert Shield/Desert Storm. Amphibious Group 2, with 4th Marine Expeditionary Brigade embarked, was stationed outside the Persian Gulf, 1,500 nautical miles from Mogadishu. (See figure.)[12]

A contingency MAGTF was formed from 4th Marine Expeditionary Brigade elements aboard the amphibious assault ship USS *Guam* (LPH 9) and amphibious transport ship USS *Trenton* (LPD 14), which set off for Somalia. The MAGTF included two squadrons of CH-46 medium transport helicopters and a detachment of two CH-53E heavy transport helicopters. The ground combat element included the Headquarters and Service Company, one rifle company, and the 81 mm mortar platoon from 1st Battalion, 2d Marines. The combat service support element included a military police platoon, landing support detachment, and medical/dental detachment that would be responsible for manning the evacuation coordination center.

Early on the morning of 5 January, at a distance of 466 nautical miles from Mogadishu, the USS *Guam* launched the two CH-53Es with a 60-man security force, including a 9-man U.S. Navy sea-air-land (SEAL) team. The flight required two aerial refuelings en route. The first guaranteed enough fuel to reach the embassy compound; the second provided enough fuel to begin the return flight to the ships.

MILITARY OPERATIONS OTHER THAN WAR

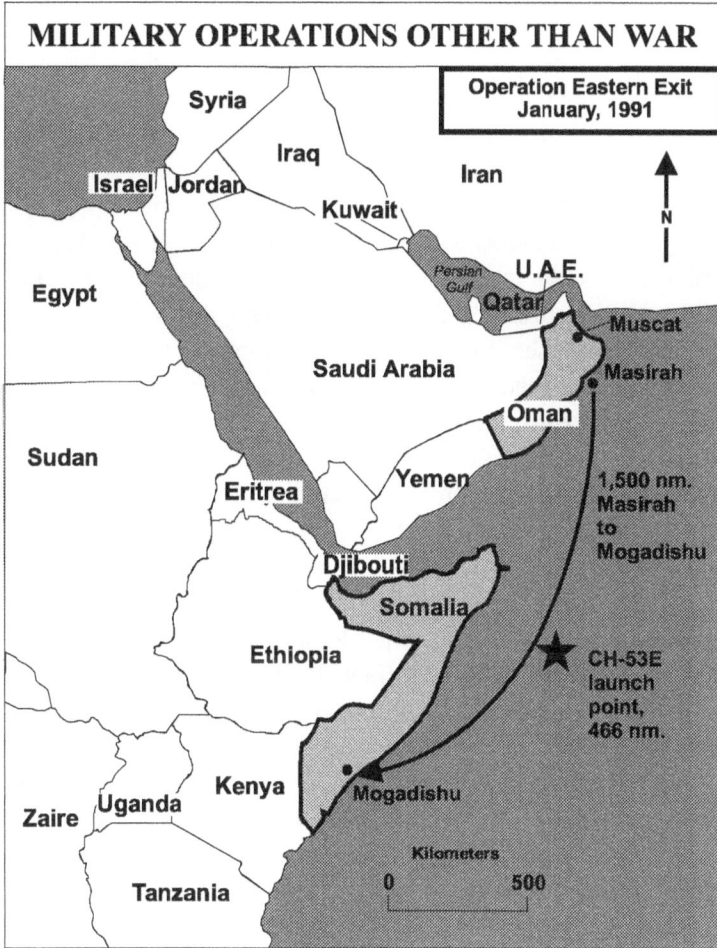

Operation Eastern Exit
January, 1991

Syria

Iraq

Israel Jordan

Iran

Kuwait

N

Egypt

Persian Gulf

U.A.E.

Qatar

Muscat

Saudi Arabia

Masirah

Oman

Sudan

Eritrea

Yemen

1,500 nm.
Masirah
to
Mogadishu

Djibouti

Somalia

Ethiopia

CH-53E
launch
point,
466 nm.

Zaire Uganda

Kenya

Mogadishu

Kilometers

0   500

Tanzania

113

CH-53Es landed at the compound at 0710. The SEAL team concentrated on protecting the ambassador at the chancery building while the Marines secured the remainder of the compound. After an hour on the ground, the CH-53Es lifted off with 61 evacuees for the return flight, with one aerial refueling, to the USS *Guam*, now 380 miles away. On the ground, the security force maintained the perimeter throughout the day. A few stray rounds impacted within the compound, but the Marines did not return fire. At one point during the day, a detachment from the security force and the embassy staff formed a convoy of hardened commercial vehicles to escort four American officials and several foreign nationals from the Office of Military Cooperation, which was several blocks away. Throughout the day, foreigners seeking evacuation arrived at the embassy.

Meanwhile, the USS *Guam* and USS *Trenton* had continued to steam at full speed toward Mogadishu, and upon arriving near the coast at 0043 on 6 January, they launched the final evacuation. This consisted of four waves of five CH-46s each. The first three waves were to evacuate civilians; the last wave would withdraw the security force. The entire CH-46 evolution was conducted using night vision goggles during the hours of darkness with the embassy compound darkened. As the last wave of CH-46s lifted off with the security force, armed looters could be seen scaling the walls of the embassy compound.

The evacuation was declared complete at 0343 on 6 January when the last CH-46 wave returned to the USS *Guam*. The ships turned north for Muscat, Oman, with 281 evacuees, including eight ambassadors, 61 Americans, and 39 Soviets. The entire expedition lasted less than 10 days. From the launch of the CH-53Es to the return of the last CH-46s, the evacuation itself had lasted less than 24 hours. On 11 January, the USS *Guam* and USS *Trenton* offloaded the evacuees in Muscat, including an infant born aboard ship, bringing the operation to a successful conclusion.

The fictional case study starting on page 125 provides an example of the possible nature and some of the challenges of future military operations other than war.

MARITIME PREPOSITIONING FORCE OPERATIONS

The concept of maritime prepositioning force operations is not an operating concept for conducting a particular expeditionary mission or category of missions. Instead, it is a deployment concept, but it is important enough as a means of rapidly providing expeditionary capability that it deserves special attention. Maritime prepositioning is not an absolute requirement for the conduct of expeditionary operations, but it figures prominently in their effective and successful execution. Maritime prepositioning force operations can support operational maneuver from the sea, sustained operations ashore, and military operations other than war. The maritime prepositioning force concept continues to evolve as new technologies improve the capabilities of the maritime prepositioning force.

A maritime prepositioning force operation is the rapid deployment and assembly of a MAGTF in a forward area using a combination of airlift and forward-deployed maritime prepositioning ships.[13] Maritime prepositioning force operations are a strategic deployment option that is global and naval in character and suitable for employment in a variety of circumstances. Maritime prepositioning provides combatant commanders with an increased capability to respond rapidly to crisis or conflict with a credible force. The purpose of a maritime prepositioning force operation is to rapidly establish in theater a MAGTF ready to conduct operations across the full operating spectrum. The strategic contribution of maritime prepositioning force operations is the rapid concentration of forces in a specified littoral region.

A maritime prepositioning force is formed when a naval force of one or more maritime prepositioning ships squadrons is united with a fly-in echelon, consisting of a MAGTF and a Navy support element. A maritime prepositioning force operation can range from one ship and an appropriately tailored fly-in echelon to all three maritime prepositioning ships squadrons and a full Marine expeditionary force. A maritime prepositioning force by itself does not possess the capability for forcible entry; it can deploy to augment forward-deployed, amphibious ready forces, which do. Maritime prepositioning force operations can also be used for missions such as occupying advanced naval bases or preemptively occupying and defending key chokepoints along sea lanes of communication. Maritime prepositioning forces are particularly well suited for supporting disaster relief and other humanitarian missions.

The pillars of future maritime prepositioning force operations are force closure, amphibious task force integration, indefinite sustainment, and reconstitution and redeployment. The futuristic case study beginning on page 125 illustrates these concepts.

Currently, maritime prepositioning forces require access to a secure port and airfield for the assembly of the force. In the future, the force-closure capability will provide for the at-sea arrival and assembly of the maritime prepositioning force. Marines will deploy via a combination of surface mobility means and strategic and theater airlift to meet underway maritime prepositioning en route to the objective area. Units will be billeted aboard the maritime prepositioning ships while readying their equipment.

Once assembled at sea, future maritime prepositioning forces will be capable of integrating with amphibious task forces. By using selective offloading to reinforce the amphibious assault echelon, the maritime prepositioning forces will be able to participate in operational maneuver from the sea. Maritime prepositioning ships will provide advanced facilities for the employment of assault support aircraft, surface assault craft, advanced amphibious assault vehicles, and the ships' organic lighterage. Further, the ships' communications systems will be fully compatible with the tactical command and control architecture of the naval expeditionary force as a whole.

Maritime prepositioning ships of the future will provide indefinite sustainment by serving as a sea-based conduit for logistics support ashore. This might be accomplished as part of a larger sea-based logistics effort which would include not only maritime prepositioning ships but also aviation logistics support ships, hospital ships, and offshore petroleum distribution systems. Maritime prepositioning ships will also be able to integrate with joint in-theater logistics agencies and to make a transition from sea-based logistics to a shore-based logistics system.

Finally, future maritime prepositioning forces will be able to conduct in-theater reconstitution and redeployment without a requirement for extensive materiel maintenance or replenishment at a strategic sustainment base. This capability to reconstitute and redeploy the maritime prepositioning force MAGTF will facilitate immediate employment in follow-on missions.

CASE STUDY: SAUDI ARABIA, 1990

The first operational use of the maritime prepositioning force concept was in the initial buildup for Operation Desert Shield in the fall of 1990.[14] The maritime prepositioning concept had been initiated in 1979 and became operational in 1984. By the summer of 1990, three maritime prepositioning ships squadrons were in service, each loaded with equipment for a Marine expeditionary brigade.

On 7 August, President Bush ordered 125,000 troops to the Persian Gulf for Operation Desert Shield. Three Marine expeditionary brigades were immediately put on alert: the 7th in California, the 1st in Hawaii, and the 4th in North Carolina. On 10 August, General H. Norman Schwarzkopf, Commander in Chief, U.S. Central Command, ordered the airlift of 1st and 7th Marine Expeditionary Brigades and the sealift of 4th Marine Expeditionary Brigade to the Persian Gulf. The 7th Marine Expeditionary Brigade would spearhead the deployment of the Central Command expeditionary force. Its ground combat element consisted of the 7th Marines (Reinforced), comprising five battalions including a light armored infantry battalion. Its aviation combat element was Marine Aircraft Group 70, consisting of fixed-wing, helicopter, air command and control, and air-defense missile units. The combat service support element was Brigade Service Support Group 7. Within 96 hours, the 7th Marine Expeditionary Brigade began embarking from air bases in southern California as the first echelon of I Marine Expeditionary Force to deploy. The U.S. Air Force's Military

119

Airlift Command flew 259 missions to deploy the personnel of the brigade.

Meanwhile, the ships of Maritime Prepositioning Ships Squadron 2 were already steaming north from Diego Garcia, in the Indian Ocean, toward the Persian Gulf.

The first troops landed at Dhahran, Saudi Arabia, on 14 August. The Marines then moved north 100 kilometers to the commercial port of Jubayl to link up with their equipment. The port was large enough to handle the simultaneous offload of an entire maritime prepositioning ships squadron. The nearby Jubayl Naval Air Facility became the aerial port of entry for most Marine personnel. Within four days of its arrival, the brigade was ready to deploy.

On 25 August, the personnel of 1st Marine Expeditionary Brigade, less its command element, started to deploy by air from Hawaii. The lead elements, two battalions from the 3d Marines, arrived at Jubayl the following day and began taking possession of the equipment provided by Maritime Prepositioning Ships Squadron 3, which had arrived from Guam the same day.

On 2 September, Lieutenant General Walter E. Boomer took command of all Marine Corps forces in theater as Commander, Marine Corps Forces Central Command, and as the commander of I Marine Expeditionary Force, which included 1st Marine Division, 3d Marine Aircraft Wing, and 1st Force

Service Support Group. The 1st and 7th Marine Expeditionary Brigades were dissolved and their forces incorporated into the elements of the Marine expeditionary force. With the dissolution of 7th Marine Expeditionary Brigade, Major General Hopkins took over as deputy commander for the Marine expeditionary force, and his staff joined the Marine expeditionary force command element.

Not all of the early deployments of Marine units were by maritime prepositioning. The 4th Marine Expeditionary Brigade deployed in early August by amphibious shipping. Along with the 13th Marine Expeditionary Unit (Special Operations Capable), already afloat, it arrived in September and became the Marine expeditionary force afloat reserve.

By the end of September, I Marine Expeditionary Force had grown to more than 30,000 Marines, Central Command's most capable combat-ready force in the theater. This was due largely to the effective first-time execution of the maritime prepositioning force concept. It had provided two-thirds of the Marine expeditionary force's combat power and supplies and had also helped sustain other forces in the theater.

CONCLUSION

Our capstone operational concept, *Operational Maneuver from the Sea*, and its supporting concepts of sustained

121

operations ashore and military operations other than war describe how MAGTFs will conduct expeditionary operations, both combat and noncombat, in response to any contingency that may be in the national interest. The maritime prepositioning force concept describes an important and proven means by which capable MAGTFs can respond quickly to crises practically anywhere in the world within a matter of days. Together these concepts describe a responsive, versatile, and reliable expeditionary capability that is invaluable in today's uncertain and turbulent world.

Epilogue

Operation Littoral Chaos

". . . there has been speculation that war itself may not have a future and is about to be replaced by economic competition among the great 'trading blocks' now forming in Europe, North America, and the Far East. This . . . view is not correct. Large-scale, conventional war—war as understood by today's principal military powers—may indeed be at its last gasp; however, war itself, war as such, is alive and kicking and about to enter a new epoch."[1]

—Martin van Creveld

T he case studies in chapter 4 provide examples of the historical application of the different expeditionary concepts. However, because of continuing doctrinal, technological, tactical, and other advancements, no historical example can do full justice to the current and future applications of those concepts. The following fictional vignette is intended to illustrate the expeditionary principles established in chapter 2 and the potential near-future application of operational maneuver from the sea and other expeditionary concepts described in chapter 4—all in a deteriorating, chaotic, political environment such as depicted in chapter 1.

CASE STUDY: WEST AFRICA, 2017–18

The West African War of 2017–18 had its origins in the collapse of civil and governmental order in the overpopulated, disease-infested slums of the African coast from Lagos in Nigeria to Conakry in Guinea. By 2017, Lagos had become the second largest city in the world with a population of some 25 million, most of them living in squalor in the burgeoning shanty slums north of the old city. Lagos had long since ceased to be under governmental control. Rule was instead divided among competing tribal groups and criminal groups with their own organized paramilitaries equipped by the growing Sudanese arms industry. A combination epidemic of malaria and HIV was the spark that ignited the war. An outbreak of malaria resistant to mefloquine necessitated treatment by blood transfusion, which accelerated the already-rapid spread of HIV. By May 2017, some health organizations were estimating the death toll from the epidemic at between a quarter and half a million. In early June, as the United Nations debated courses of action, mass violence erupted between Muslim Hausa and Fulani tribes on the one hand and Christian Yorubas and Ibos on the other in the disease-infested suburban slums of Ikeja and Mushin. The tribal violence quickly spread westward, engulfing Benin and Togo by mid-June. Within two weeks, riotous violence had turned into organized military action as Military Coalition of West African Governments peacekeeping forces, unpaid for months, were quickly bought off by one or the other of the opposing factions.

On 10 June, the United Nations passed an emergency resolution asking member nations to send immediate military assistance and humanitarian aid to the region. The U.S. Commander-in-Chief, Europe (CINCEUR), would command what would eventually become a 15-nation coalition. The U.S. contingent to the multinational force was designated as Joint Task Force 405.

The 22d Marine Expeditionary Unit (special operations capable), stationed offshore on forward-deployment since late May, landed in the early morning of 12 June. (See figure.) Escorted by their organic short takeoff and vertical landing joint strike fighters (STOVL JSFs), the Marine Expeditionary Unit's (special operations capable) MV-22s transported

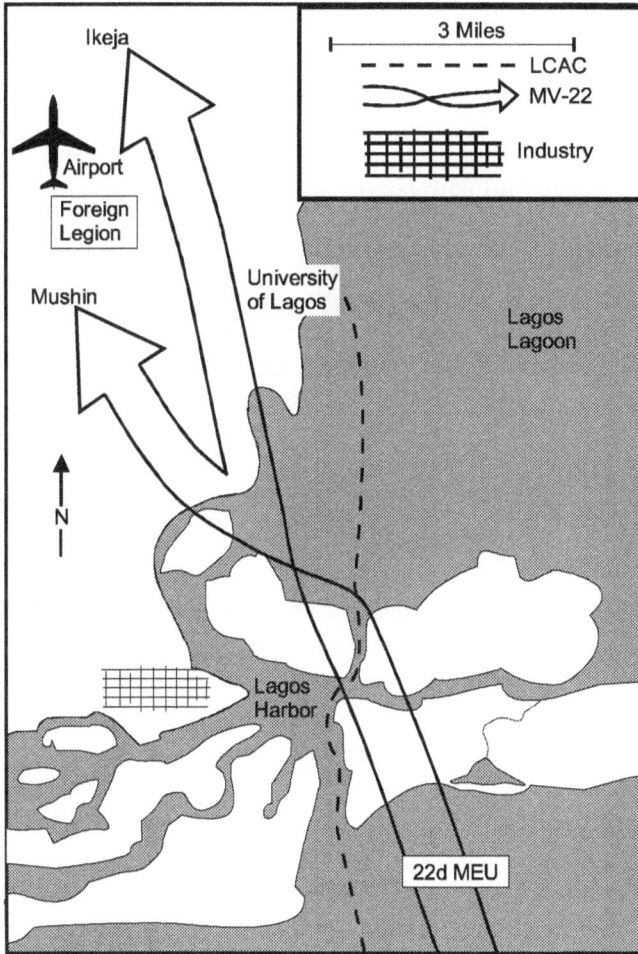

Lagos, June 2017.

Marine forces directly to objectives near Mushin and Ikeja, while surfaceborne elements moved by advanced amphibious assault vehicles (AAAV) and air-cushion landing craft (LCAC) through the narrow Lagos Harbor into Lagos Lagoon, bypassing the industrial city and landing instead near the campus of the University of Lagos, a hotbed of unrest. On the same day, a battalion of the French Foreign Legion deployed to Lagos by air but was diverted to Ilorin some 300 kilometers to the north until the Marine expeditionary unit could secure Lagos' Murtala Muhammed Airport the following day. After a week of continuous patrolling in the face of intermittent resistance, Marine and Foreign Legion forces restored some semblance of order to the northern suburbs of Lagos. Malaria was so pervasive that parts of the city had to be quarantined. Marines and Legionnaires were billeted aboard U.S. Navy ships and were ferried back and forth by MV-22.

Also on 12 June, Maritime Prepositioning Ships (MPS) Squadron 1, stationed in the Mediterranean, headed for the scene via the Strait of Gibraltar. The squadron included two newly commissioned enhanced maritime prepositioning ships designed to augment amphibious operations. (See figure.)

On 22 June the ready brigade of the 82d Airborne Division began to arrive by air at Abidjan, Ivory Coast, to perform humanitarian aid and peacekeeping missions. In late June and early July, forces from France, Great Britain, Italy, Angola, and South Africa began arriving at coastal cities to perform similar missions. On 26 June, Regimental Landing Team 2 and

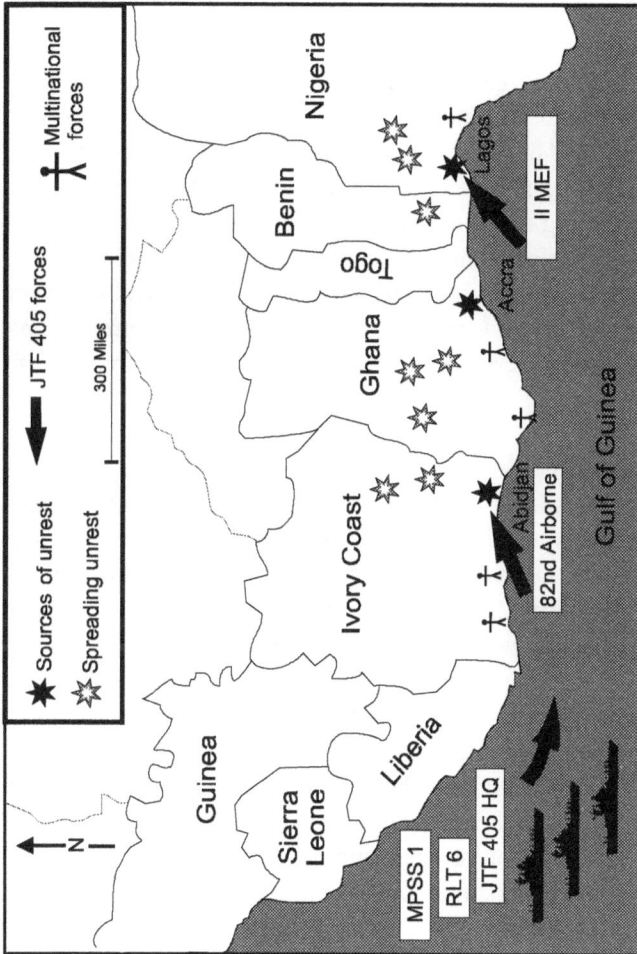

Force deployment, Summer 2017.

other elements of II Marine Expeditionary Force deployed by amphibious shipping from North Carolina. Meanwhile, Regimental Landing Team 6 deployed by commercial and military airlift to Douala, Cameroon, to link up by MV-22 with MPS Squadron 1. The II Marine Expeditionary Force commenced peacemaking and peacekeeping operations in Lagos in early July, absorbing the 22d Marine Expeditionary Unit (special operations capable). Using decentralized tactics developed over the previous two decades, the Marines systematically cleared the cramped urban terrain of resistance through aggressive patrolling and a series of isolated small-unit combined-arms actions.

Joining Joint Task Force 405 from the United States were an aviation logistics support ship to provide sea-based aviation support and a hospital ship to provide a floating disease treatment center. Digitally connected to disease specialists in the United States, medical personnel afloat were eventually able to get the epidemic under control by autumn.

Meanwhile, various groups took advantage of the unrest to advance their own interests. On 29 June, Muslim-backed forces fighting for the People's Dahomian Nation (PDN) shelled Accra, Ghana, as fighting continued westward. Fighting also began to move inland as opposing armies fought for control of Nigerian and Ghanian oil and mineral fields. Abidjan was overrun by refugees fleeing the fighting, and the city nearly doubled in population, to nearly three million, in the span of a month.

Overwhelmed by starvation and disease, Abidjan quickly became a disaster area.

One of the greatest threats to expeditionary forces ashore was malaria which threatened the operational effectiveness of several units, including one Italian battalion that suffered 40 percent casualties due to the disease. Reports of anthrax usage by the warring factions in several cities could not be confirmed because some urban areas were essentially inaccessible. A more common threat to United Nations forces was the use of "Lagos smokers," crude chemical devices that upon impact produced toxic fumes by mixing potassium cyanide with acid. Delivered by hand or by rocket, these simple but effective weapons could produce mass casualties and could leave an area uninhabitable for days. Initially, these were employed primarily against civilian populations, but soon they were used increasingly against United Nations forces and facilities by both Muslim and Christian factions. By mid-August, Marine patrols were routinely operating in protective gear, and that same month, the chemical-biological incident response team from Marine Corps Forces Atlantic deployed to Lagos. Due to the chemical threat, several United Nations positions ashore became untenable and had to be withdrawn in August and September to ships of MPS Squadron 1, which thereafter provided permanent sea bases and billeting for several United Nations units. In September, MPS Squadron 2 deployed from Diego Garcia via the Cape of Good Hope to provide additional sea-basing support for U.S. and United Nations forces.

In August the westward expansion of fighting had halted east of Abidjan, now held in force by the 82d Airborne Division. The war entered a positional phase which lasted for the next 6 months as Muslim and Christian forces regularly launched rocket and artillery attacks against each other, civilian populations, and occasionally United Nations forces. By late September, some relief organizations estimated total casualties due to military action and disease at over 750,000. On 21 September, with organized violence on the rise again, the United Nations Security Council passed a resolution expanding the charter of coalition forces, authorizing them to use military force to disarm any military or paramilitary forces in the field. Over the next 4 months the 22d Marine Expeditionary Unit (special operations capable), designed as the Joint Task Force 405 amphibious strike force, conducted six amphibious raids against Muslim or Christian positions in the Ivory Coast to a range of up to 250 kilometers inland.

In March 2018, the course of the war changed dramatically when the National Liberian People's Front (NLPF), out of power some 15 years, launched a successful coup in Monrovia, Liberia, supported by units from the army of Sierra Leone. (See figure.) The coup was coordinated with a renewed offensive by the PDN that threatened to eliminate organized Christian opposition in Ghana and Nigeria. The NLPF and PDN followed the coup in Liberia with a campaign of genocide aimed at Christian and animist tribes in Liberia, Ghana, and Nigeria.

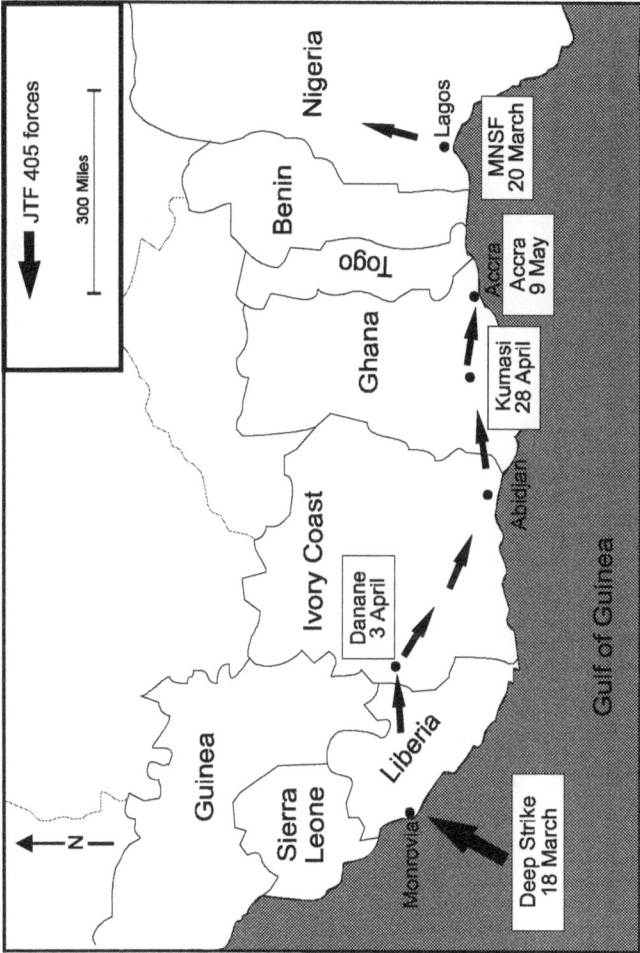

In mid-March, the 22d Marine Expeditionary Unit (special operations capable) was designated Special Purpose MAGTF Deep Strike and was reinforced with the 2d Light Armored Reconnaissance (LAR) Battalion (already deployed to Lagos), 1st LAR Battalion (deploying by air from Camp Pendleton, California, to link up with selected ships of MPS Squadrons 1 and 2), and a squadron of attack helicopters with organic ground aviation support. The ground combat element came ashore at Monrovia from maritime prepositioning and amphibious ships on 18 March, met sporadic resistance, and struck immediately inland against the NLPF and PDN. Two days later a French-led Multinational Strike Force struck from the United Nations lodgment in Nigeria to destroy PDN forces in the field there.

In conjunction with air strikes and MV-22 attacks against targets in the enemy rear, the light armor battalions of Deep Strike drove inland under orders "to defeat NLPF forces and stop the tribal slaughter." MAGTF fixed- and rotary wing aviation assets conducted urban offensive air support throughout the area of operations. Dense civilian populations made target discrimination difficult, but accurate overhead imagery provided by organic unmanned aerial vehicles and low-yield precision-guided munitions fired by fixed- and rotary wing assets greatly reduced that problem. After continuous skirmishing, the decisive battle occurred outside Danane, Ivory Coast, on 3 April, and remaining NLPF forces surrendered near Daloa on 11 April. The Deep Strike ground forces continued on to Abidjan, linking up with the 82nd Airborne and their own sea-based support on 13 April. On 20 April, the replenished ground combat element struck inland again, this time against

PDN forces in the Ivory Coast and Ghana, reaching Kumasi on 28 April and the Ghanian coast on the eastern outskirts of Accra on 9 May. Supported entirely from the sea by naval long-range fires, STOVL JSFs, MV-22s, and other assault support aircraft, Special Purpose MAGTF Deep Strike ground units had maneuvered some 1,400 kilometers in the 6-week operation. By this time the Multinational Strike Force had defeated PDN forces in Nigeria and advanced as far west as Cotonou, Benin. On 10 May, the U.S. Commander-in-Chief, Europe, ordered offensive operations halted, putting an end to major military operations in the war, although peacekeeping and humanitarian aid operations continued.

The special purpose MAGTF deployed home in late May, followed by II Marine Expeditionary Force. Starting with the 24th Marine Expeditionary Unit (special operations capable) in early June, a forward-deployed Marine expeditionary unit remained nearby for the next 18 months. With the situation ashore stabilized, and under the protection of a permanent United Nations observation force, relief organizations began returning in the early summer of 2018.

CONCLUSION

In addition to illustrating future operational maneuver from the sea, this fictional case study also shows the key implementing concepts of ship-to-objective maneuver, maritime prepositioning, and sea basing in a chaotic littoral environment. Landing forces use enhanced tactical and operational mobility to avoid enemy defenses and maneuver directly against operational objectives without first establishing a beachhead. Maritime prepositioning forces, using at-sea arrival and assembly capabilities, are integrated into the amphibious task force. Landing forces sustained and supported from the sea enjoy increased freedom of action by eliminating the need to establish and protect a large support base ashore.

The Landscape: Chaos in the Littorals

1. Niccolò Machiavelli, *The Prince*, trans. Luigi Ricci (New York: Mentor Books, 1952) p. 55.

2. Robert D. Kaplan, *The Ends of the Earth: A Journey at the Dawn of the 21st Century* (New York: Random House, 1996) p. 10.

3. Samuel P. Huntington, "The Clash of Civilizations?" *Foreign Affairs* (Summer 1993) pp. 22–49.

4. U.S. Congress. Senate. Senate Select Committee on Intelligence. *Global Threats and Challenges to the United States and Its Interests Abroad.* Statement presented by LtGen Patrick M. Hughes, U.S. Army, Director, Defense Intelligence Agency, to the 105th Cong., 1st Sess., 5 February 1977.

5. Kaplan, p. 8.

6. **Crisis**: "An incident or situation involving a threat to the United States, its territories, citizens, military forces, possessions, or vital interests that develops rapidly and creates a condition of such diplomatic, economic, political, or military importance that commitment of U.S. military forces and resources is contemplated to achieve national objectives." (Joint Pub 1-02)

7. MCIA-1586-001-97, *Marine Corps Midrange Threat Estimate—1997–2007: Finding Order in Chaos* (Quantico, VA: Marine Corps Intelligence Activity, August 1996) p. 1.

8.   Dr. James N. Rosenau, "Fragmegrative Challenges to National Security," in *Understanding U.S. Strategy: A Reader,* ed. Terry L. Heyns (Washington, D.C.: National Defense University Press, 1983) pp. 65–82.

9.   MCIA-1586-001-97, p. 11.

10.   Ibid., pp. 14–15 and 42–43.

11.   Charles William Maynes, "Relearning Intervention," *Foreign Policy* (Spring 1995) p. 108.

12.   MCIA-1586-001-97, p. 2.

13.   Ibid.

14.   Ibid.

15.   Ibid., p. 3.

16.   *World Resources 1996–97* (New York: Oxford University Press, 1996) p. ix.

17.   MCIA-1586-001-97, p. 8.

18.   *World Resources 1996–97*, pp. 58–59.

19.   Ibid., p. 9.

20.   Eric Grove, *The Future of Sea Power* (London: Routledge, 1990) p. 31.

21.   Ibid., p. 46.

22.   MCIA-1586-001-97, pp. 1 and 3.

23.   *World Resources 1996–97*, pp. 60–61.

24.   The five permanent members of the United Nations Security Council—the United States, Russia, the United Kingdom, France, and the People's Republic of China—are all declared nuclear powers. India, Pakistan, and Israel are known to possess nuclear weapons. North Korea and Iraq have had confirmed nuclear weapons production programs, and Iran is suspected of conducting nuclear weapons research. Politicians in Taiwan have expressed an interest in developing nuclear weapons, and South Korea had official plans to develop nuclear weapons as late as 1991. South Africa, Argentina, and Brazil have all renounced their nuclear weapons programs but have the technological capability to resume them at any time. Essentially any group with a technological capability equivalent to that of the United States in the 1960s could design a nuclear weapon. MCIA-1586-001-97, p. 15.

The Nature of Expeditionary Operations

1.   Sir Julian Corbett, *Some Principles of Maritime Strategy* (Annapolis, MD: Naval Institute Press, 1988) p. 16.

2.   Lowell Thomas, *Old Gimlet Eye: The Adventures of Smedley D. Butler* (New York: Farrar & Rinehart, 1933) p. 127.

3.   U.S. President. *A National Security Strategy for a New Century* (Washington, D.C.: The White House, Office of the President of the United States, May 1997) pp. 14–15.

4.   **Expedition**: "A military operation conducted by an armed force to accomplish a specific objective in a foreign country." (Joint Pub 1-02)

5.   **Force**: "1. An aggregation of military personnel, weapon systems, vehicles, and necessary support, or combination thereof." (Joint Pub 1-02)

6.   **Logistics**: "The science of planning and carrying out the movement and maintenance of forces." (Joint Pub 1-02)

7.   F. G. Hoffman, "Advanced Expeditionary Warfare–2015" (unpublished draft concept paper, Marine Corps Combat Development Command, Studies and Analysis Division, Quantico, VA, 1996).

8.   The Marine Corps no longer employs the Marine expeditionary brigade organization. A Marine expeditionary brigade was roughly one-third the size of a Marine expeditionary force and comprised a permanent command element and units from one of the standing Marine expeditionary forces. These brigade command elements are no longer in existence.

9.   Robert Debs Heinl, Jr., Col, USMC, Retired, *Dictionary of Military and Naval Quotations* (Annapolis, MD: United States Naval Institute, 1966) p. 11.

10. This responsibility is assigned to the Marine Corps by United States Code, Title 10, chapter 503, section 5013, with the following words: "The Marine Corps shall develop, in coordination with the Army and the Air Force, those phases of amphibious operations that pertain to the tactics, techniques, and equipment used by landing forces."

11. **Strategic mobility**: "The capability to deploy and sustain military forces worldwide in support of national strategy." (Joint Pub 1-02)

12. **Sustainability**: "The ability to maintain the necessary level and duration of operational activity to achieve military objectives. Sustainability is a function of providing for and maintaining those levels of ready forces, materiel, and consumables necessary to support military effort." (Joint Pub 1-02)

Expeditionary Organizations

1. Quoted in Robert D. Heinl, Jr., Col, USMC, Retired, *The Marine Officer's Guide* (Annapolis, MD: Naval Institute Press, 1977) p. 71.

2. Quoted in Robert D. Heinl, Jr., Col., USMC, Retired, *Victory at High Tide: The Inchon-Seoul Campaign* (Baltimore, MD: The Nautical & Aviation Publishing Company of America, 1979) pp. 6–7.

3. **Expeditionary force**: "An armed force organized to accomplish a specific objective in a foreign country." (Joint Pub 1-02)

4.   **Landing force**: "A task organization of troop units, aviation and ground, assigned to an amphibious assault. It is the highest troop echelon in the amphibious operation." (Joint Pub 1-02)

5.   "Department of the Navy 1997 Posture Statement," *Marine Corps Gazette* (April 1997) p. 14, excerpt from a report by the Honorable John H. Dalton, Adm Jay L. Johnson, and Gen Charles C. Krulak.

6.   **Fleet Marine Force**: "A balanced force of combined arms comprising land, air, and service elements of the U.S. Marine Corps. A Fleet Marine Force is an integral part of a U.S. Fleet and has the status of a type command." (Joint Pub 1-02)

7.   The force that conducted Operation Eastern Exit was at the time called a "contingency MAGTF," a term no longer in use.

8.   **Service component command**: "A command consisting of the Service component commander and all those Service forces, such as individuals, units, detachments, organizations, and installations under the command, including the support forces, that have been assigned to a combatant command, or further assigned to a subordinate unified command or joint task force." (Joint Pub 1-02)

9.   **Functional component command**: "A command normally, but not necessarily, composed of forces of two or more Military Departments which may be established across the range of military operations to perform particular operational missions that may be of short duration or may extend over a period of time." (Joint Pub 1-02)

Expeditionary Concepts

1.   Quoted in Heinl, *Victory at High Tide*, p. xv.

2.   Quoted in *Assault From the Sea: Essays on the History of Amphibious Warfare*, ed. Merrill L. Bartlett, LtCol USMC, Retired (Annapolis, MD: United States Naval Institute, 1983) p. xi.

3.   *Operational Maneuver from the Sea*, (Quantico, VA: Marine Corps Combat Development Command, Concepts Division, 1996) PCN 145 000001 00.

4.   **Amphibious operation**: "An attack launched from the sea by naval and landing forces embarked in ships or craft involving a landing on a hostile or potentially hostile shore." (Joint Pub 1-02)

5.   For the history of Operation Forager, see Henry I. Shaw, Bernard C. Nalty, and Edwin T. Turnbladh, *Central Pacific Drive*, History of U.S. Marine Corps Operations in World War II, vol. III (Washington, D.C.: Headquarters, U. S. Marine Corps, Historical Branch, 1966) pp. 231–585; Jeter A. Isely and Philip A. Crowl, *The U.S. Marines and Amphibious War: Its Theory, and Its Practice in the Pacific* (Princeton, NJ: Princeton University Press, 1951) pp. 320–371; and FMFRP 12-109, *The Amphibians Came to Conquer: The Story of Admiral Richmond Kelly Turner*, vol II (September, 1991) pp. 853–968.

6.   This case study is taken primarily from Col Charles J. Quilter, *U.S. Marines in the Persian Gulf, 1990–1991: With the I Marine Expeditionary Force in Desert Shield and Desert Storm* (Washington, D.C.: Headquarters, U.S. Marine Corps, History and

Museums Division, 1993). See also J. Robert Moskin, *The U.S. Marine Corps Story* (Boston: Little, Brown and Co., 1992).

7. Quilter, pp. 73–74.

8. Ibid., p. 76.

9 Ibid., p. 102.

10. **Military operations other than war:** "Operations that encompass the use of military capabilities across the range of military operations short of war. These military actions can be applied to complement any combination of the other instruments of national power and occur before, during, and after war." (Joint Pub 1-02). According to Joint Pub 3-07, *Joint Doctrine for Military Operations Other Than War* (June 1995), the 16 types of military operations other than war are: arms control, combatting terrorism, DOD support to counterdrug operations, enforcement of sanctions/maritime intercept operations, enforcing exclusion zones, ensuring freedom of navigation and overflight, humanitarian assistance, military support to civil authorities, nation assistance/support to counterinsurgency, noncombatant evacuation operations, peace operations, protection of shipping, recovery operations, show of force operations, strikes and raids, and support to insurgency. This listing of military operations other than war is somewhat misleading in that many of the operations included in this category, for example strikes and raids, clearly fall within the classical definition of war.

11. The definitive treatment of Operation Eastern Exit is Adam B. Siegel, *Eastern Exit: The Noncombatant Evacuation*

Operation (NEO) from Mogadishu, Somalia, in January 1991 (Alexandria, VA: Center for Naval Analysis, 1991). See also Adam B. Siegel, "Lessons Learned From Operation EASTERN EXIT," *Marine Corps Gazette*, June 1992, pp. 75–81.

12. Siegel, "Lessons From Operation EASTERN EXIT," June 1992, p. 77.

13. FMFM 5-1, *Maritime Prepositioning Force Operations* (October 1993) p. 1-1.

14. This case study is taken primarily from Quilter.

Operation Littoral Chaos

1. Martin van Creveld, *The Transformation of War* (New York: The Free Press, 1991) p. 2.

www.ingramcontent.com/pod-product-compliance
Lightning Source LLC
Chambersburg PA
CBHW021336090426
42742CB00008B/623